THE MUSICAL EXPERIENCE

ORIGINALLY PUBLISHED BY
PRINCETON UNIVERSITY PRESS

ROGER SESSIONS

THE
MUSICAL
EXPERIENCE
OF
COMPOSER,
PERFORMER,
LISTENER

ATHENEUM   NEW YORK

1962

Published by Atheneum
Reprinted by arrangement with
Princeton University Press

PREFACE

THE present volume consists of a set of six lectures delivered, in the summer of 1949, at the Juilliard School of Music, New York City. A few very minor changes, including a rearrangement of some of the material of the first lecture, have been made in the text.

I wish to acknowledge with gratitude the valuable help of my wife and of Miss Evelyn Leloff, who typed the original manuscript; of Professors Edward T. Cone and Roy Dickinson Welch, and Miss Margot Cutter, all of whom made valuable suggestions regarding the final form of the text; and finally of my pupil Mr. Robert Helps, who has been of the greatest assistance in correcting the proofs.

For the title "The Musical Experience" I am indebted to my friend and former pupil Mr. Andrew Imbrie.

ROGER SESSIONS

Berkeley, California
May 1950

CONTENTS

THE MUSICAL EXPERIENCE

I

The Musical Impulse

How shall we explain the power that men and women of all times have recognized in music, or account for the enormous importance they have ascribed to it? Why did primitive peoples endow it with supernatural force and create legends, persisting into times and places far from primitive, in which musicians of surpassing ability were able to tame wild beasts, to move stones, and to soften the hard hearts of gods, demons, and even human tyrants? Why have serious and gifted men—in imaginative force and intellectual mastery the equals of any that ever lived— why have such men at all periods devoted their lives to music and found in it a surpemely satisfying medium of expression?

Music, of all the arts, seems to be the most remote from the ordinary concerns and preoccupations of people; of all things created by man, its utility, as that word is generally understood, is least easy to demonstrate. Yet it is considered among the really important manifestations of our western culture, and possibly the one manifestation in which our western contribution has been unique. Those who have created its lasting values are honored as among the truly great. We defend our convictions concerning it with the utmost intensity; and at least in some parts of the world we bitterly excoriate those whose convictions differ, or seem to differ, from our own. We regard music as important, as vitally connected with our-

3

selves and our fate as human beings. But what is the nature of our vital connection with it? What has impelled men to create music? What, in other words, are the sources of the musical impulse? I would like to explore here some approaches to an answer to this question.

Our way will be easier, I think, if we ask ourselves first: is music a matter of tones sung or played, or should we consider it rather from the standpoint of the listener? A close examination of this question leads to some rather surprising conclusions. We find that listening to music, as we understand it, is a relatively late, a relatively sophisticated, and even a rather artificial means of access to it, and that even until fairly recent times composers presumably did not think of their music primarily as being listened to, but rather as being played and sung, or at most as being heard incidentally as a part of an occasion, of which the center of attention for those who heard it lay elsewhere than in the qualities of the music as such.

In fact, composer, performer, and listener can, without undue exaggeration, be regarded not only as three types or degrees of relationship to music, but also as three successive stages of specialization. In the beginning, no doubt, the three were one. Music was vocal or instrumental improvisation; and while there were those who did not perform, and who therefore heard music, they were not listeners in our modern sense of the word. They heard the sounds as part of a ritual, a drama, or an epic narrative, and accepted it in its purely incidental or symbolic function, subordinate to the occasion of which it was a part. Music, in and for itself can hardly be said to have existed, and whatever individual character it may have had was essentially irrelevant.

Later, however, as certain patterns became fixed or traditional, the functions of composer and performer began to be differentiated. The composer existed precisely because he had introduced into the raw material of sound and rhythm patterns that became recognizable and therefore capable of repetition—which is only another way of saying that composers began to exist when music began to take shape. The composer began to emerge as a differentiated type exactly at the moment that a bit of musical material took on a form that its producer felt impelled to repeat.

The same event produced the performer in his separate function; the first performer was, in the strictest sense, the first musician who played or sang something that had been played or sung before. His type became more pronounced in the individual who first played or sang music composed by someone other than himself. At both of these points the performer's problems began to emerge, and whether or not he was aware of the fact, his problems and his characteristic solutions and points of view began to appear at the same time. These will be discussed in detail later on. Here it is important only to envisage clearly that the differentiation of composer and performer represents already a second stage in the development of musical sophistication. The high degree of differentiation reached in the course of the development of music should not obscure the fact that in the last analysis composer and performer are not only collaborators in a common enterprise but participants in an essentially single experience.

I am not, of course, talking in terms of musical history. The developments I have cited are not in any precise sense historical, and I have not presented them as hypothetically so. It would certainly be in accordance with historical fact, however, to think of them as a long, somewhat involved, gradual development, of which I have given a condensed and symbolical account. And this very qualification underlines better the point I am making: namely, that the performer, as distinct from the composer, is the product of already advanced musical refinement. While the relationship of the composer to music is a simple, direct, and primary one, that of the performer is already complex and even problematical. To be sure, the composer as an individual may be the most complex of creatures and the performer the simplest—I have personally known examples of both such types! But while the act of composition, of production, is a primary act, that of performance—that is, re-production —is already removed by one step. The music passes through the medium of a second personality, and necessarily undergoes something of what we call interpretation. I am not raising here the much discussed question of what interpretation is, or what it may or should be; whether it should be "personal" or object-tive," whether it can be or should be historically accurate, and so forth. I am simply pointing to it as an inevitable aspect of the performer's activity, of which the other aspect is, of course, projection. The performer, in other words, not only interprets or re-conceives the work, but, so to speak, processes it in terms of a specific occasion: he projects it as part of a recitation or a concert, as the embodiment of a dramatic moment or situation, a part of a ritual, or finally and perhaps most simply as a piece performed solely for his own delectation. Whether or not he is aware of the fact, the nature of his performance is conditioned by the circumstances under which it takes place.

It hardly need be pointed out that the relation to music of the listener is even more complex than that of the performer. As I have pointed out, the listener, as we think of him today, came fairly recently on the musical scene. Listening to music, as distinct from re-producing it, is the product of a very late stage in musical sophistication, and it might with reason be maintained that the listener has existed as such only for about three hundred and fifty years. The composers of the Middle Ages and the Renaissance composed their music for church services and for secular occasions, where it was accepted as part of the general background, in much the same manner as were the frescoes decorating the church walls or the sculptures adorning the public buildings. Or else they composed it for amateurs, who had received musical training as a part of general education, and whose relationship with it was that of the performer responding to it through active participation in its production. Even well into the nineteenth century the musical public consisted largely of people whose primary contact with music was through playing or singing in the privacy of their own homes. For them concerts were in a certain sense occasional rituals which they attended as adepts, and they were the better equipped as listeners because of their experience in participating, however humbly and however inadequately, in the actual process of musical production. By the "listener," I do not mean the person who simply hears music—who is present when it is performed and who, in a general way, may either enjoy or dislike it, but who is in no sense a real participant in it. To listen implies rather a real participation, a real response, a real sharing in the work of the composer and of the performer, and a greater or less degree of awareness of the individual and specific sense of the music performed. For the listener, in this sense, music is no longer an incident or an adjunct but an independent and self-sufficient medium of expression. His ideal aim is to apprehend to the fullest and most complete possible extent the musical utterance of the composer as the performer delivers it to him.

And how, through what means, does he do this? Let

us think for a moment of a similar instance of artistic experience, which is however not quite so complex in structure. The reader of a poem does not generally receive the poem through the medium of an interpreter, nor does he, generally, actually "perform," i.e. read aloud, the poem himself. Yet the rhymes and the meters, as well as the sense of the words, are as vivid to him as they would be if the poem were actually read to or by him. What he does in fact is to "perform" it in imagination, imaginatively to re-create and re-experience it. The "listener" to music does fundamentally the same thing. In "following" a performance, he recreates it and makes it his own. He really listens precisely to the degree that he does this, and really hears to precisely the extent that he does it successfully.

I have discussed this question in some detail here not in order either to belittle the listener or to minimize the validity or the intensity of his relationship to music. What I do wish to point out is that if we are to get at the sources of the musical impulse, we must start with the impulse to make music; it is not a question of why music appeals to us, but why men and women in every generation have been impelled to create it. I have tried to show as clearly as possible that composer, performer, and listener each fulfill one of three separate functions in a total creative process, which was originally undifferentiated and which still is essentially indivisible. It is true that there are listeners—as, alas, there are composers and performers! —of every degree of talent and achievement. But the essential is that music is an activity: it is something done, an experience lived through, with varying intensity, by composer, performer, and listener alike.

An understanding of these matters will help us to seek and perhaps to understand the basic facts regarding the musical impulse. We will know better, for instance, than to seek them in the science of acoustics or even primarily with reference to sounds heard.

Let me make this a little clearer. A great deal of musical theory has been formulated by attempting to codify laws governing musical sound and musical rhythm, and from these to deduce musical principles. Sometimes these principles are even deduced from what we know of the physical nature of sound, and as a result are given what seems to me an essentially specious validity. I say "essentially specious" because while the physical facts are clear enough, there are always gaps, incomplete or unconvincing transitions, left between the realm of physics and the realm of musical experience, even if we leave "art" out of account. Many ingenious and even brilliant attempts, it is true, have been made to bridge these gaps. One of the difficulties of trying to do so, however, is apparent, in the way in which the physical fact of the overtone series has been used by various harmonic theorists to support very different and even diametrically contradictory ideas. Because the first six partial tones obviously correspond exactly with the tones composing the major triad, theorists are fond of calling the latter the "chord of nature." On that premise, Heinrich Schenker, for example, a brilliant and at times profound writer, has reconstructed the theory of tonality as basically an elaboration of that chord or its "artificial" counterpart, the minor triad. He bases what he considers the immutable laws of music on these deductions, even though in doing so he virtually excludes the music written before Bach, after Brahms, and outside of a rather narrowly Germanic orbit. Furthermore, what is perhaps even more problematical, he is forced to disregard the evolutionary factors within even those limits, and to regard the musical language of Bach and Mozart and Beethoven and Brahms in exactly the same light; and he remonstrates with even those composers whenever he catches them punching holes in the system he has thus established. Or again, Paul Hindemith, also a brilliant and certainly a more creative writer, has carefully examined the overtone series and made very interesting deductions regarding it, but he gives it an even more outspoken status than has Schenker, as a kind of musical court of last appeal, with the triad as final arbiter, on the basis not of musical experience, but of physical science. Other writers, however, noting that the overtone series extends well beyond the first six partials, have found in this fact justification for harmonic daring of a much more far-reaching type, and have in some cases sought to discover new harmonic principles based on the systematic use of these upper partials.

Such speculations have been in many cases the product of brilliant minds, of indisputable musical authority, and I do not wish in any way to minimize this fact. Yet it would be easy to point out that each author, in a manner quite consistent with his musical stature, found in the overtone series a tool he could adapt to his individual and peculiar purpose. Above all it seems to me clear that physics and music are different spheres, and that, though they certainly touch at moments, the connection between them is an occasional and circumstantial, not an essential, one. For the musician at any level of sophistication, it is his experience, his relationship with sound, not the physical properties of sound as such, which constitute his materials. Experience, and only experience, has always been his point of departure, and while it has often led him to results which find apparent confirmation in the non-human world, this is by no means always the case. Even when it is the case, it can be regarded as no more than an interesting coincidence until a clear connection with musical experience can be demonstrated.

What I wish to stress is the fact that since music is created by human beings, we must regard the sources, or raw materials, first of all as human facts. For it is not rhythm and sound as such but their nature as human facts which concerns us. And if we look at them closely we perceive that they are actually human facts of the most intimate kind. We see that these basic facts —the raw materials, the primitive sources, of music— are facts of musical experience and not the physical facts of sound and rhythm.

Let us look at rhythm first, since it is perhaps the primary fact. It is quite customary to refer our feeling for rhythm to the many rhythmical impressions constantly received from experience—the non-human as well as the human, the subconscious as well as those of which we are aware, and the sophisticated and complex as well as the naïve and simple. Reference is made not only to the act of breathing and walking, but to the alternation of day and night, the precession of the equinoxes, and the movement of the tides; to the beating of the heart, to the dance, and to many another instance of rhythmic recurrence in nature and man, even the mechanical rhythms which everywhere impose themselves on our consciousness. Such illustrations certainly have their place and their relevance; anything so fundamental as our rhythmic sense certainly is nourished and no doubt refined by impressions of every kind, and I believe we may truly say that it remains impervious actually to none. It seems to me also, however, that such generalizations miss a fundamental point. For our rhythmic sense is based ultimately on something far more potent than mere observation.

It seems to me clear indeed that the basic rhythmic fact is not the fact simply of alternation, but of a specific type of alternation with which we are familiar from the first movement of our existence as separate beings. We celebrate that event by drawing a breath, which is required of us if existence is to be realized. The drawing of the breath is an act of cumulation, of tension which is then released by the alternative act of exhalation.

Is it, then, in any way far-fetched to say that our first effective experience of rhythm, and the one that remains most deeply and constantly with us, is characterized not only by alternation as such, but by the alternation of cumulative tension with its release in a complementary movement? This is, actually, the primary fact of musical rhythm too. We recognize it in the technical terms "up-beat" and "down-beat," arsis and thesis; and we apply it, consciously as well as instinctively, to our conception of larger musical structure, as well as to the more familiar matters of detail to which these terms are generally applied.

What, for instance, is a so-called "musical phrase" if not the portion of music that must be performed, so to speak, without letting go, or, figuratively, in a single breath? The phrase is a constant movement toward a goal—the cadence; and the rhythmic nature of the latter is admirably characterized in the term itself, derived from the Italian verb *cadere*, to fall: that is, the "falling" or down-beat, the movement of release.

I am tempted to call this the most important musical fact, and am sure I have done so on occasion. More than any other fact, it seems to me, it bears on the nature of what I shall call "musical movement"; on it depends the appropriateness to their context of harmonies, of melodic intervals, and details of rhythmic elaboration. From it are derived the principles on which satisfactory musical articulation is based; and many an otherwise excellent performance is ruined through inadequate attention to what it implies. How often, unfortunately, in the performance of music, do we hear so much emphasis put on the first part of the phrase that its conclusion is left dangling in the air! The phrase does not, if I may put it that way, sit: the effect is one of breathlessness because the tension is not quite released, or to put it a little differently, the goal of the phrase is not clearly felt. It is not a question of what is generally called accent, but rather of solidity and firmness.

For instance, I have sometimes been distressed to hear the following passages from Beethoven's Quartets played thus:

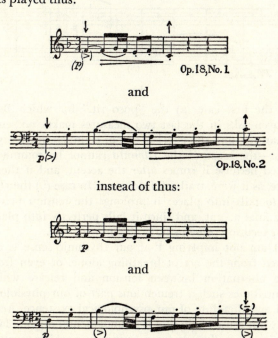

Op.18, No.1

and

Op.18, No.2

instead of thus:

and

Or, still more distressingly, I have heard the opening of the Scherzo of Beethoven's Fifth Symphony played thus:

(a)

instead of, correctly, thus:

(b)

In the first case (a) the "poco rit." for which Beethoven asks in the last two measures makes no sense
whatever, and the effect is one of complete indecisive-
ness—the sense of the *ritenuto* cannot be communicated because it comes *after* the accent, and it therefore, as it were, trails off into space. In case (b) the *ritenuto* falls into place: it prolongs the tension before
the final accent, and since it falls perfectly into place,
its execution presents no problems whatever.

I am not implying that our rhythmic sense is derived from the act of breathing alone, or even from
the alternation between tension and release which
contributes such a tremendous part of our physiologi-
cal and therefore of our psychological existence. Actually our sense of rhythm is a fundamental organic fact,
the product of many forces within us working together
toward a common end. Nor have I forgotten that the
term "rhythm" is often used in an inclusive sense, em-
bracing not only the facts I have described, but what
we define more strictly as tempo and meter as well.

Once more I should like to emphasize that it is through our perception of these elements, our awareness of them, that they have meaning for us, and that we gain this perception through the experiences of our pyscho-physical organism. Here it is not a question of the alternation of tension and relaxation but of our experience of time itself. We gain our experience, our sensation of time, through movement, and it is movement, primarily, which gives it content for us. It is unnecessary to seek scientific proof of this. We need only a clear analysis of ordinary experience, and it is the latter, in any case, which is relevant to the nature of music. We judge tempo first of all by the relation of basic metrical pulsations to the speed with which we accomplish the ordinary actions of our existence, such as walking and speaking; but, in a more extended sense, we judge it by the amount of effort required to reproduce or respond to it. Heavy accents call forth more energy because we subconsciously assume more energy in producing them; they suggest, and therefore actually call forth in our imagination, greater effort, of which the physiology can be demonstrated many times and in many contexts. Similarly, music rich in detail or elaboration, whether melodic, rhythmic, harmonic, or polyphonic, requires greater effort on the part of the hearer than when the changes are less constant or the detail less elaborate. Consequently music of the former type performed at a fast tempo will seem energetic and strained, while music of simple texture may move along, however rapidly, with the utmost ease and grace.

Nietzsche, always a profound writer on music though not himself a musician, laments in his *Jenseits von Gut und Böse* ("Beyond Good and Evil") the passing of what he calls the "good old time" of Mozart and Haydn, when, to paraphrase his words, a true Presto movement was possible in music.

He cites Mendelssohn as the last composer who could write a real Presto. To be sure, he did not know Verdi's "Falstaff"; and needless to say, he was speaking of the music of genuine composers and not of imitators of past styles. Everything, he said, had become ponderous, heavy in spirit, and weighted down with preoccupation; a vital ease had disappeared from the life and hence the culture of Europe. Leaving aside his psychological judgment, which does not concern us at this point, and translating his statements into analytic terms, is he not drawing true conclusions from the indisputable fact that the music of the nineteenth century was, actually, far richer in texture and in coloring than that which had preceded it, and that this fact in itself precluded the type of movement which Haydn embodied so often in his Finales, or Mozart in such a work as the Overture to "The Marriage of Figaro," in which detail is reduced to a minimum of elaboration, and contrasts are of the subtlest kind?

These few observations lay no claim to exhaustiveness. The subject of rhythm is a vast one, and indeed an adequate definition of rhythm comes close to defining music itself. It is a subject, too, that lends itself all too easily to oversimplification, a clear case of this being the abstraction of the rhythmic element in music from that of musical sound.

Now, if we consider musical sound from the standpoint of the impulse to produce it, we find that in a very real sense and to a very real degree this impulse, too, is rooted in our earliest, most constantly present and most intimate experiences. From almost the first moments of our existence the impulse to produce vocal sound is a familiar one, almost as familiar as the impulse to breathe, though not so indispensable. The sound, to be sure, is at first presumably a by-product. But is it not clear that much of our melodic feeling derives from this source; that is, from a vocal impulse which first of all is connected with the vital act of breathing and is subject to its nuances? In the second place melodic feeling undergoes vast refinement during the growth of even the most unmusical individuals. From the vocal impulse we acquire, for instance, our sensitive response to differences in pitch. I mean here powers not of discrimination, but of response, the kind of response that is instinctive and that precedes discrimination and possibly even precedes consciousness. In simple terms, when we raise our voices we increase the intensity of our vocal effort, a rise in pitch implies an increase in tension, and therefore an intensity of energy, or, in other terms, of expressiveness in one direction. When we lower our voices we make a different kind of effort, and gain an intensity of a different and more complex kind. Similarly, an increase in volume denotes, not only in terms of the physical effort of production, but in the sympathetic effort of response, also an increase in tension and hence of intensity. I have spoken of intensity of expression, which of course is synonymous or commensurable with the degree of contrast involved. If we like, we may speculate on the combinations possible between two directions of movement of pitch, and two directions of movement in volume. We may try to formulate, for instance, the effect of high or rising notes sung or played very softly, or of a descending passage sung or played crescendo. What I believe will be indisputable is the fact that with only slight qualifications we carry over these primitive responses from music produced vocally to our more complex response to that heard instrumentally, independently of the particular character of the instrument involved. Though subject to definition, qualification, and refinement, it is a very basic musical response of which I am speaking, and possibly more

17

than any single factor it governs our response to melody in its largest features. I shall discuss actual discrimination, the refined sense of pitch, later; here I am referring to the purely instinctive bases of musical expression, as nearly as I can define them, quite apart from the coordinative function of the musical ear. It is true that the line of demarcation is an arbitrary one. But the discrimination of delicate shades of difference in pitch, such as all civilized musical systems demand, only refines these basic responses. It makes possible, through the fact of notes of fixed and definite pitch, greater precision in rhythmic and melodic contour.

Nevertheless, a melodic motif or phrase is in essence and origin a vocal gesture; it is a vocal movement with a clearly defined and therefore clearly expressed profile. And, one final point, it too is sensitive to infinitely delicate nuances of tension and relaxation, as these are embodied in the breathing which animates the vocal gesture and shapes its contours. Thus, agitated breathing will be reflected in agitated melodic and rhythmic movement; or conversely, sharp, irregular accents, or successive violent contrasts in pitch will call forth subconscious associations suggesting the kind of agitation which produces violent or irregular breathing, just as quieter melodic movement will evoke a more serene response.

I am oversimplifying, of course. These are not the only elements in musical expression, but I am deliberately restricting the discussion here to primitive, direct, and simple responses to music. Even at this level, may we not say that the basic ingredient of music is not so much sound as movement, conceived in the terms I have indicated? I would even go a step farther, and say that music is significant for us as human beings principally because it embodies movement of a specifically human type that goes to the roots of our being and takes shape in the inner gestures which embody our deepest and most intimate responses. This is of itself not yet art; it is not yet even language. But it is the material of which musical art is made, and to which musical art gives significance.

If we appreciate these facts, we can understand the more readily why music is the art of sound. For of all the five senses, the sense of hearing is the only one inexorably associated with our sense of time. The gestures which music embodies are, after all, invisible gestures; one may almost define them as consisting of movement in the abstract, movement which exists in time but not in space, movement, in fact, which gives time its meaning and its significance for us. If this is true, then sound is its predestined vehicle. For what we apprehend through the eye is for us static, monumental. Even movement seen is bounded by our range of vision; we never can closely follow it off into space unless we ourselves move. Sound, at least in our experience, is never static, but invariably impermanent; it either ceases or changes. By its very nature it embodies for us movement in time, and as such imposes no inherent limits.

To sum up: the experience of music is essentially indivisible, whether it is embodied in the impulse to produce, or in the response, through re-production, actual as by the performer or imaginary as by the listener, of the musical experience embodied in music already produced. Secondly, what we may call the raw, formal materials of music are also the expressive elements, and these, again, have their basis in certain of the most elementary, intimate, and vital experience through which we live as human beings. Let us consider now the means through which these raw materials are coordinated, become coherent, and are rendered significant; through which, in other words, they begin to be music.

II

The "Musical Ear"

IN THE last chapter I discussed what I may perhaps call the roots of our musical feeling—roots lying in the very depths of our nature as animate beings. Here I should like to stress the vast sweep of the topmost branches of the tree that has grown from these roots.

My metaphor, I believe, is not a bad one. For it emphasizes a fact we ought never to forget: that a genuine culture is an organic growth, and not a self-conscious achievement. Possibly we Americans especially need to remember this. We are aware, quite aside from any self-congratulatory spirit, of having accomplished a very great deal in a very short time, and we tend sometimes to minimize all that is implied in the growth from roots to topmost branches; to seek short cuts that would make this arduous process unnecessary. One of our characteristic traits is a combination of naïveté and sophistication, with a quite considerable degree of both; and, in consequence, some uncertainty as to whether we really wish to be the one or the other. The danger, of course, is that our sophistication loses contact so easily with its roots that it becomes cautious and genteel instead of earthy and secure; it becomes critical instead of creative in character. That is one reason I have laid such stress on the roots, on primitive musical feeling. When our musical response penetrates strongly down to that level, or rather—to preserve my metaphor—when it penetrates up from it, discrimination follows

almost automatically, and with our instinct sure, our response can be untroubled. I would, of course, go much farther than this and say that the only kind of discrimination that is very real or very trustworthy is formed in this way; that is, on the basis of a strong and vital response to music on the deep level I have spoken of.

If we retain awareness of the roots of our musical impulses, we can give them their due importance without crediting them with telling the whole story. Music has at all times, and above all in our own, fulfilled a variety of functions and provided satisfactions of different kinds, some of them seemingly far removed from the instinctual level. At all periods, for instance, we find music in which the associative element is strong, whether the latter arises from a text which is sung, or from a "program" which is more or less naïvely illustrated by the music. In fact musically uneducated people often think this is the only type of music, and assume that only associative musical expression is authentic. But before discussing authentic musical expression, let us consider for a moment what the basic impulses, as described in the last chapter, really imply in terms of the word expression. Does music express emotion or does it merely arouse it?

As happens so often in speaking of music, the facts are much simpler than the words found to describe them. No one denies that music arouses emotions, nor do most people deny that the values of music are both qualitatively and quantitatively connected with the emotions it arouses. Yet it is not easy to say just what this connection is. If we try to define the emotions aroused by specific pieces of music, we run into difficulties. I have referred elsewhere to cases in which the emotions purportedly expressed in a given work have been defined by different musicians in quite different terms. For instance, Beethoven's Seventh Symphony has been described by three composers, including Berlioz and Wagner, as "heroic" or "warlike," as "pastoral," or as the "apotheosis of the dance." This is a celebrated example, since two composers of genius and many musicians of lesser stature have been articulate about it. But you have only to read the various interpretative comments on almost any well-known work to find the same result.

Does this mean that the "message" or "emotional content" of music is an illusion, and that actually a given piece of music conveys one thing to one man, another thing to another, and that our illusion of specific emotional content derives entirely from the quite adventitious associations which we are able to bring to it? I do not believe this for a moment and I thoroughly dislike the terms, indeed the whole jargon, in general use. On the contrary, I believe that music "expresses" something very definite, and that it expresses it in the most precise way. In embodying movement, in the most subtle and most delicate manner possible, it communicates the attitudes inherent in, and implied by, that movement; its speed, its energy, its élan or impulse, its tenseness or relaxation, its agitation or its tranquility, its decisiveness or its hesitation. It communicates in a marvelously vivid and exact way the dynamics and the abstract qualities of emotion, but any specific emotional content the composer wishes to give to it must be furnished, as it were, from without, by means of an associative program. Music not only "expresses" movement, but embodies, defines, and qualifies it. Each musical phrase is a unique gesture and through the cumulative effect of such gestures we gain a clear sense of a quality of feeling behind them. But unless the composer directs our associations along definite lines, as composers of all times, to be sure, have frequently done, it will be the individual imagination of the listener, and not the music itself, which defines the emotion. What the music does is to animate the emotion; the music, in other words, develops and moves on a level that is essentially below the level of conscious emotion. Its realm is that of emotional energy rather than that of emotion in the specific sense.

Does all this imply, as is from time to time intimated, that music is a vague and imprecise means of communication? I have frequently heard such views expressed, especially by people working primarily in other media, and most often by literary people. They hold that music expresses nothing definite, and that it is therefore only a more or less pleasant form of self-indulgence, in fact a rather harmful one, since, to paraphrase such statements, it stimulates day-dreaming, arouses emotions for which it provides no outlets in the real world, and indeed should be considered a kind of drug—a symptom, even an agent, of a decadent rather than a healthy culture. This obviously raises a fundamental question, and one with more aspects than appear at first glance but which will be referred to frequently later on. At present, I am concerned with only one of them—the question of communication. Does music actually communicate something it is capable of defining clearly?

It seems to me quite clear that music, far from being in any sense vague or imprecise, is within its own sphere the most precise possible language. I have tried to imply this by saying that music embodies a certain type of movement rather than that it expresses it. All of the elements of this movement— rhythm, tempo, pitch, accent, dynamic shading, tone quality, and others sometimes even more subtle—are, in competent hands, kept under the most exquisite control, by composer and performer alike; the movement that is the stuff of music is given the most precise possible shape. It was for just this reason that both the ancients and the teachers of the Middle Ages accorded to music such high place in educational discipline. By these means, a musical gesture gains what we sometimes call "musical sense." It achieves a meaning which can be conveyed in no other way. When, according to a well-known and possibly true anecdote, Beethoven in answer to a query as to the "meaning" of his Eroica Symphony turned to the piano and played the first bars of the work, he was, in effect, not only implying that its message could not be conveyed in any other way; he was also, and at least as clearly, implying that that message was something quite exact and precise, embodied in the tones, rhythms, harmonies, and dynamics of the passage.

The confusion concerning music as a means of communication clearly arises from a lack of understanding of what music really signifies. If we try to qualify the meaning of a piece or a passage of music in terms of specific emotions, we immediately run into the difficulties of which I have already spoken. Not only do we find the music essentially indefinable, but the more precisely we try to define it, the more unsatisfactory the result. What we achieve fails to be convincing as a true description of the music; and it becomes clear immediately that the music does not rouse the same specific feelings in different individuals—in fact, it does not define feelings at all. Once more, music embodies the attitudes and gestures behind feelings—the movements, as I have said, of our inner being, which animate our emotions and give them their dynamic content. Each of us qualifies these attitudes and gestures according to the associations that our experience has provided. Something similar happens, to be sure, even when words are provided. Take the Pastoral Symphony, for example. The countryside Beethoven saw in imagination was an Austrian countryside, the brook flowed down a slope near Vienna, the birds—cuckoo, quail, and nightingale— are specific European birds, quite recognizable if somewhat stylized. I have long since ceased visualizing in connection with music, but if I ever did, my landscape was, because I spent my boyhood in New England, a flat, lush valley, my brook ran straight and across meadows, and the cuckoo, quail, and nightingale were abstractly conceived bird-sounds which it would have seemed quite pointless to identify. Yet the tranquil and even static placidity of the first movement, the gently rippling flow of the second, and so forth—the real sensations conveyed by Beethoven—were, as they still are, completely specific, and completely indescribable in words.

We can approach the question from another position, also. We may consider what elements in a given medium are kept under direct control, and which are left comparatively free. In music, rhythm, tempo, dynamic intensity, as well as pitch and every nuance of harmony, are controlled with the utmost precision while specific association is at most conveyed through words sung, images evoked by the help of a program, or drama as made visible on the stage. The gesture and the inflection are definite; the sense in terms of images and associations is free; the inflection and gesture are perhaps the more definite for being given the full weight of the expression. With words —poetry or literature—it is the gesture and inflection that are left comparatively free. Rhythm is controlled only in a very general sense; it is subject to the widest possible variety of interpretation without fear of distortion. The same phrase or sentence may actually be read in a number of different ways without destroying its real meaning. This is true in music only within very narrow limits. Even when the greatest freedom is accorded to the interpreter, metric time

25

values must be preserved; musicians argue bitterly over relatively small differences in tempo, and the composer takes the trouble to indicate as clearly as possible exactly what he wants. The same is true in regard to articulation, dynamic shading, accent, and, obviously, pitch and tone quality. The point is that in music it is the gesture and the inflection that are expressive, therefore definite and controlled to the most minute degree of refinement. The gesture is, in other words, in the foreground, whereas in literature, the words in their specific sense, evocative, associative, and even sonorous, bear the expressive burden. One must not demand from one medium what can be better and more efficiently furnished by another.

Of course, artists will extract from their respective media whatever resources these seem capable of yielding; and not only in music do we find them adopting, on occasion, sources of expression that have little to do with those on which their particular art is based. Actually, what I may call associative expression in music is not, in its pure form, so common as is sometimes assumed; most often it consists in association through movement, which is, as I have pointed out, the very stuff of musical expression. The composer in such cases fixes the listener's response to a specific set of associations, and in some cases the associations even contribute a certain measure of coherence that the music by itself fails to provide.

Nevertheless, we are all familiar with other, more literal and occasionally more naïve types of associative suggestion—naïve, and sometimes even quite far-fetched. When Strauss symbolizes and also qualifies scientific "learning" by means of a very intricate fugue, he actually is demanding quite a measure of such "learning" of the hearer: the ability to follow, or at least to recognize a fugue even though the subject is slow, complex, and played pianissimo in the lowest register; he is also assuming that the hearer associates the fugue with a measure of dry and intricate technical exercise. And yet this is not quite all that the passage contains: the music can also be listened to without thought of the "program" attached to it; it has both expression and movement of a type that might easily be qualified in terms fairly remote from the program Strauss has indicated. An even more problematical instance is that of the composers of the Renaissance who set such passages in their texts as referred to "darkness," either literal or figurative, by using in their manuscript short notes, which, like our quarters, eighths, sixteenths, and so forth, as against our "white" half and whole notes, were literally black, and hence "darkened" the page.

Never, as far as I know, has the attempt at associative suggestion in music been carried to more far-fetched conclusions, and it is clear that this type of suggestion is as irrelevant as it is out-dated. What is interesting is that in spite of such irrelevances of attitude and practice, the music was so often musically expressive, just as I have indicated in the case of Strauss. It tends to demonstrate what in fact I have been trying to show, that the essential musical fact lies precisely in the gesture which animates and not in the idea or context which defines our feelings.

Music, then, is a language—that is, a means of communication, and what it communicates is perfectly definite and clear. We shall discuss later on the means through which music becomes an art—that is, the means through which this communication becomes significant. But first let us consider a little further the means by which communication is actually effected, and by which it is apprehended.

I often wonder how many of us stop to think of what a complex of functions we include in the term "ear" in referring to musical perception or musical ability. There are certainly current, apart from musically informed people, many grotesque misapprehensions of what the "ear" really means. I remember a gathering, mainly of literary people, in which I was taken to task for implying quite casually that the sound of an orchestral score, and the possible interpretations of that score, could be quite vivid to me through reading the notes, even if I had neither heard the score performed nor played the notes myself. Such a claim seemed to them more than miraculous and they regarded as impossibly arrogant, not to say fraudulent, my claim that I was the seeming miracle man who could accomplish it, even though they themselves would not have accepted even as mildly humorous a suggestion that perhaps they ought to read their poems aloud in order to make sure that the rhymes were correct!

Actually the auditory functions possessed by the musician, even the musical genius, are possessed by the human race as a whole; they are not the peculiar property of musically gifted people nor are they, some educational theorists to the contrary notwithstanding, indications or criteria of musical ability. The musician has to develop them, it is true; their development to a high degree is indispensable to him, and this development is also favored by his predilections and by the sensibility which those predilections develop. But what mature and experienced musician has not known individuals with the truest sense of auditory discrimination who nevertheless remain quite impervious to music, and unable either to love or understand it? On the other hand, which one of us has not known musicians of outstanding and even superlative ability who have been, at some point in their career, hampered by deficiencies such as difficulty in reading at sight or in composing without the help of the piano, handicaps they have been obliged to overcome by dint of the utmost drudgery? I am not, of course, referring to Beethoven's deafness. In the real sense of the word, Beethoven was never deaf, and the musical world perhaps would have been spared many grotesque errors regarding his later music if this fact had been understood earlier; for since his "deafness" was for many years used as a convenient means of dodging the problem posed by his music for performer and the listener alike, this misconception postponed the day when performers began to cope with those problems. What was insufficiently realized was that Beethoven, even at the time of the onset of his physical deafness, had passed well beyond the stage demanded of an average pupil. He was able to hear sounds imaginatively or, as we sometimes say, "internally" quite as well as anyone. I believe few people any longer dispute that his musical imagination not only grew in force, but developed new technical resources demanded by his creative powers, precisely during the years of his almost total physical deafness. The latter had, let us say, deprived him of a tool he no longer needed; and it is idle to speculate on whether his music would have been different had he been able to hear it. The answer is that possibly he himself would have been different; and that if his music had been different it would have been for this reason, and not primarily because he retained the faculty of physically hearing sounds which he was capable of hearing, with the utmost vividness, in imagination.

One cannot, therefore, combat too sharply the notion that the purely material manifestations of the musical accomplishment count most decisively. The story that Mozart composed the overture of "Don Giovanni" the night before the première is, I believe, apocryphal; certainly several aspects of it make it incredible. But even if it is granted to be true, the miracle is the overture to "Don Giovanni" itself, a miraculous piece of music, and not any circumstances which may or may not have attended its composition. It is characteristic, indeed, of the true composer that his music, while he is composing it, is constantly in his mind, always and everywhere, and that it is never a matter simply of a task accomplished during working hours, however regular these may be. The music derives whatever vitality and whatever depth it may possess partly from that very fact; for this means that the composer identifies himself with it, lives it to the fullest extent, and that in this way he gives to it his complete self, the sum and the best of his faculties, and not a detached part of them.

The musical ear, then, discriminates; and this is the first of its functions, a basic and indispensable one. Its indispensability is proportionate to the needs, both professional and personal, of the musician or the listener. It identifies sounds in all of their aspects: their pitch, their tone quality, their relative intensity, their mode of production, their duration. It becomes, as I have already implied, a more than purely auditory function, in identifying and responding to the basic rhythmic facts; tempo, meter, and that alternation of tension and release which is the essence of rhythm proper. It is these elements, highly developed as they must become for the musician, that excite popular wonder and are so often regarded as indicative of phenomenal talent. Actually, as I have indicated, they are only the beginning, for the real role of the musical ear is to organize musical sensations. The ear not only discriminates; it associates and coordinates musical impressions. It creates, discovers, or becomes and remains aware of relationships between sounds, between musical ideas, and between rhythmic accents, motifs, phrases, periods, sections, movements. In the largest sense it develops into what I shall later call musical imagination; but prior to that stage it fulfills a complex, indispensable, and not always clearly understood function.

It will perhaps have been noticed that while I have spoken of rhythm and of melody, and the basis of each, on the impulsive level, I have not spoken as yet of that aspect which is generally ranked with rhythm and melody as the third basic element of music: harmony. The reason I have not done so is that I envisage harmony as primarily a coordinative element and not, like rhythm or melody, an impulsive one. I do not mean by that to draw a distinction between "form" and "content" or "form" and "expression" —and I think you will see, I do not believe in such a distinction. The words thus brought into opposition are in no way opposed, and when art is in a quite healthy state they are identical. But though harmony becomes eventually a vehicle for expression, it does so first of all in its character as an organizing force, and secondarily in its function of organizing contrasts.

Let me first define briefly what I mean by harmony in this context, for the term is either so often taken to imply chords, sonorities, either literally expressed or implicit; or else it is strictly associated with the specific idea of tonality. I am using it here in no such restricted sense, but to refer to the whole factor in music of which the above are instances; i.e. the relationships between tones, and above all, the organization which the ear deduces, let us say, from those relationships. Thus, while it is in one sense both quite correct and quite logical to say that the strictly harmonic sense developed only during the latter part of the sixteenth century, this would refer to a set of facts other than the ones I am now considering. It is during that period, roughly speaking, that composers became harmonically self-conscious, that what we call

the vertical sense, the feeling for chords as such and
not as results of good voice-leading, began to develop
as a recognized new dimension and new means of
expression—that is, a new resource having possi
bilities of development within itself. But before that
for many centuries and long before the use of two or
more notes simultaneously, musicians were aware of
intervals, of unity in the purely melodic sphere. This
in fact, was one of the principal problems with which
musical theorists grappled, and the musical theorists
habit, mentioned in the last chapter, of referring to
the overtone series actually dates back from possibly
five hundred to four thousand years. The early theo
rists, whether Greek or Chinese, found the overtone
series very useful in establishing norms of pitch rela
tionship, of scale structure, and the like. Their rela
tionship to it was a very practical one, partly because
it served the purpose of establishing a norm and
partly because, whatever the reason, the octave and
the fifth became for them, as they have remained for
us, the simplest of intervals. These were relationship
so fundamental that they became, even in the earlies
times, decisive in the organization of tones—point
of reference, that is, or premises, around which the
organization of tones was accomplished. While I am
not going to give a detailed account of this organiza
tion or to try to relate the functions of these tone
to the facts of harmony as we know them today,
do wish to point out that the ancients were already
aware of the octave and the fifth as facts and as bind
ing forces.

The intervals of the octave and the fifth, and to
some degree also the fourth, thus became in very early
days factors of an elementary harmonic nature. The
limited and defined the space within which, accord
ing to the current mode of hearing, melody could co

herently move, and enabled the ear to recognize these as constant and fixed relationships. Since this is not a course in harmonic theory, only two very basic points are important. The first of these is that the ear learned at a very early stage not only to discriminate between tones and to identify and measure intervals, but to become aware of differences in character between them, and even to learn to classify them in a functional sense. In this respect the ear was aided by the facts of vocal tone production, and the psychological impact of these facts. It noted that the larger the interval, the greater effort required to sing it, and also that certain intervals, irrespective of the foregoing, were far more difficult to sing than others. The second point is that certain intervals, partly, no doubt, because they were easier to produce, established themselves as, so to speak, binding forces. The ear discovered that two notes an octave or a fifth apart tended to associate themselves in a kind of binding pattern even if other notes came between them; that the impressions fused in a unifying framework, within or around which other notes tended to fall into their appointed places. They tended, that is, to form clearly intelligible patterns and to provide a basis of reference whereby patterns of sound could be given intelligible and clearly recognizable shape. A melody thus became a precisely and clearly outlined musical entity, one which could be recognized and exactly repeated. Finally, it became clear that the various tones of the scale within a firm modal framework were different in function and in effect because of their place within that framework. In other words, the ear, through the logical elaboration of its own impulses and demands, gradually discovered or created a system of relationships which enabled it to hear coherent patterns of sound and rhythm. It learned to extend those relationships, to absorb into the system even more far-flung relationships in a manner which I shall presently try to indicate.

In a sense, of course, these facts are the ones which every student of harmony learns in his first lessons—the facts of consonance and dissonance, of scales and modes. But it is worthwhile to consider that they represent actually a very complex development and one which throws light on the essential nature of our relationship to music. It helps us to understand, for instance, that the musical ear is not a passive function, which simply registers or even, so to speak, merely draws patterns of tonal sensation, but is one which feels and thinks, which constantly seeks new relations and develops new resources in the service of musical expression.

So, later, it became inevitable that musicians should investigate the possibilities yielded by the sounding of tones simultaneously. No doubt, though I believe it would be hard to demonstrate, the earlier experiences summarized here were necessary as preparations for this stage of development. The development of the conceptions of consonance and dissonance in respect to simultaneous sounds follows logically from the processes I have indicated. The intervals that were most clearly available as binding tones in the earlier logic of melody were first to emerge as acceptable intervals when sung or played simultaneously. The ear, in other words, became aware of, understood, or assimilated most easily the relation of the octave, the fifth, and the fourth, and only gradually and later incorporated into its system the other intervals: the thirds and the sixths, the sevenths and seconds, and finally the augmented and diminished intervals. We are familiar, if we know our music history, with the struggles which attended each new conquest; and we should have learned also not to confuse, as did some of our nineteenth century predecessors, the development of the musical language with the quite different idea of progress in musical art. But at the same time, we, who live in what has every aspect of a transitional period of culture in general and of music in particular, should try to understand what has produced this transitional period, and not be tempted, as all too many of us actually are, into an attitude of pessimism and implicit despair by the fact that we have difficult problems to solve. For those problems, though certainly difficult in the extreme, are inherently of exactly the same nature as those faced by former periods; and if we can retain our spirits before them, such pessimism will appear not only thoroughly destructive, but essentially unjustified. The problems require our best efforts, that is all.

The use of harmonic intervals led to an entirely new plane of relationships. Eventually the resulting complexes of sound, or as we call them, chords, were discovered to imply relationships between themselves, and the relationships between chords, as composers became aware of them, led to the awareness of a quite new set of principles or, as it sometimes seems, a new dimension in music. This new dimension, tonality, made possible first of all the literal transposition of musical phrases and harmonies from one pitch to another. Perhaps its greatest significance lies in this fact. Before its discovery, or perhaps we should rather say, its development, the problem of what we call key never arose because the fact of modulation did not exist. A degree of contrast was obtainable by the use of different modes, with their varied cadences; but this never assumed the character of modulation until, by a process of evolution, which we will not describe in detail here, the modes evolved, or crystallized, into two basic types: the major and minor. Modulation was made possible by the fact that in actual practice the mode constructed on, for instance, F came more and more closely to resemble that constructed on C, and that constructed on D or E became nearly identical with that on A.

To illustrate: The medieval "Ionian" mode corresponded to our scale of C major; the "Aeolian" mode with our "pure" or "natural" minor scale of A. The "Dorian" mode was based on the tone D, the "Phrygian" on E, the "Lydian" on F, and the "Mixolydian" on G. Composers eventually came to feel the need, at each cadence, of approaching the final tone always from its lower semitone, and accordingly established the custom of raising the seventh degree of each of the scales in which the seventh degree lay a whole tone below the principal tone.

In order to avoid the dissonant "augmented second" which resulted from this procedure, in the Phrygian and Aeolian modes, they also raised the sixth degree at points where this tone preceded the raised seventh. These two procedures resulted in the following:

Aeolian
(A minor, ascending)

Dorian
(D minor, ascending)

Mixolydian
(G major)

Phrygian
*(E minor, ascending, *with "Phrygian" second degree)*

* The "Phrygian" second has left many traces in musical usage

36

As for the "Lydian" mode, the fourth was very frequently lowered in order to avoid the dissonant "augmented fourth" or "tritone" F-B. Thus

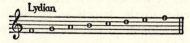

tended to become

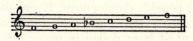

or F major.

The result was the possibility of transposition, that is, the setting up of associations implying relationships of a new kind and of larger and wider dimensions. The older relationships were, so to speak, extended. The relationship, to take one instance, of the notes C—G, had evolved first to the relationship of the chords C—G; and this had in time become extended farther, making possible what we call the key relationship C—G.

I am not going to carry this particular line of development farther at this point, because, first, what I have been saying is intended primarily as an illustration of the way in which the musical ear functions as a coordinator of musical impressions, as well as of the extraordinary range of its power of coordination. Secondly, I think it will be well if at this point we stop to consider briefly some of the results of the processes I have described. I have spoken of extension. This word

---

of "baroque" and "classic" times and later, and must be regarded as a regular and frequently used variant of the minor second degree. In practice the seventh (hence also the sixth) degree was, in this mode far oftener than in the others, frequently left unaltered. When the altered seventh occurred, the second degree was also, frequently though not invariably, raised a semitone in order to avoid the resulting dissonance.

is applicable not only to the ever-widening circle of relationships between notes, but also to the extension of musical materials in terms of possible length and development. A musical idea, taking the term in its broadest sense, carries largely within itself the seeds of its own development, and the greater the circle of possible relationships—between notes, later between chords, still later between keys—the more extended the area of possible development. Hence the development of tonality was a necessary condition for the development of large design in music, since tonality alone provided an adequate means of contrast. Until a tonal center could be radically shifted, the extension of musical form was hampered by the fact that a single tonal center tended to grow monotonous and wearisome. Since, as we have seen, the very nature of music is time, the result of successive impressions, contrast of the type yielded by tonality becomes indispensable if the music is to last more than a very short time.

Secondly, tonality implies a kind of perspective in sound, sometimes compared rather shrewdly to perspective in visual art. For it makes possible a system of relationships which are unequal in strength, in emphasis, or in significance, and the setting off of musical episodes through placing them tonally in relationship to this system. All of the so-called "standard" forms are primarily illustrations of this fact. The principal sections of a fugue, a rondo, of a sonata, are identified with the principal key, and the contrasting sections derive a large measure of their varying degrees of contrast from the relationship of the keys in which they are set to the main tonal center. I hardly need point out that the best composers of the eighteenth and nineteenth centuries learned to use these resources with the utmost mastery, flexibility, and expressive power.

Let us leave the subject of harmony here for the

moment. The new developments brought, as we all know, by the nineteenth and twentieth centuries must be reserved for later reference. My purpose here has been to give some illustration of what the musical ear is, and the way it functions. We have seen that it coordinates musical impressions by perceiving and utilizing relationships between tones, and that where used creatively it constructs musical edifices out of these relationships. It may be worthwhile now to indicate very briefly the means through which it does this, and through which we may be sure that different hearers hear fundamentally the same things; that they get the same musical sense from the same work or performance.

The ear coordinates impressions by reducing them always to their simplest relationships, by seeing (or rather hearing) them always in the simplest light. Perhaps the best illustration is the fact that if we hear a single note in the absence of association, or a single consonant chord, our ear will always assume that it is the tonic, the principal or conclusive note of the key; and we will retain this impression until the composer, by setting up another relationship, forces us to revise it. Likewise, over a fairly long stretch of music we hear by selecting from our impressions those tones or chords which are thrown into strong relief by the rhythmic and harmonic structure and relating them to each other on the first level. It is by this means that a composer makes his structure clear, and by this means that the hearer apprehends it. Each relies, that is, on the selective and the coordinative function of the ear, which coordinates impressions by reducing them to the simplest forms. We have been discussing the nature of the musical ear on the very generalized level of musical materials in the abstract. The activity of the ear does not end here. It organizes not only the generalized rhythmic, melodic, and harmonic materi-

als, but the specific musical ideas of the composer—
the motifs, phrases, harmonic and rhythmic patterns
which constitute his individual materials and that of
the particular musical work. As I have deferred discussion of the harmonic language of the nineteenth
century and of today because it leads into regions
which require a high degree of definition and which
themselves lead into the realms of the speculative and
problematic, so shall I defer these other questions, as
being closely bound up with the work of the composer
in its individual and creative aspects and inseparable
from them.

So far I have tried to indicate the factors and the
means through which music becomes a language—
that is, a means of communication. I have tried to
show what is the essential nature of its message—that
is, the substance which it communicates—and the
means through which that communication is effected.
I hope in the following chapters to indicate some of
the means through which it becomes art—coordinated
and significant communication—and some aspects of
its condition in the world today.

III

The Composer

I HAVE said that music, especially today, fulfills a variety of functions and exercises a variety of appeals. I do not mean to imply that this has not always been the case. It seems to me, however, that it must be much more so today than ever before. Not only do we have music written for the church and music for secular occasions; we also have music written for educational purposes; we have "popular" music for all sorts of purposes, and so-called "classical" music of all types. We have music written for symphony orchestras and music written for amateurs, music written frankly for its own sake and music written with an eye to "audience appeal" of a very particular kind. Note that I have not spoken of the various "tendencies" to which the sophisticates like to refer, but rather to functions and, by implication, basic purposes of composers. I wish the above facts were more clearly understood, or at least that conclusions were more clearly drawn from them.

Unfortunately, we have to some extent acquired a wholly artificial set of standards, which confuses functions with values—a really serious confusion, leading to many misunderstandings. It would be such a good thing if we would take more note of the fact that, for instance, a good piece of popular music has a far better chance for what we call "immortality" than a bad symphony; that the two belong to different categories which make quite different demands, and fulfill quite different functions, each having its inevitable and presumably legitimate place in our cultural life. Each category contains its own particular types of good and bad music. The good music demands in each case the complete participation of those whose talents and inclinations place them in that particular category; and it seems fairly clear that composers only fail if they try to meet the demands of basic categories other than the ones to which they properly belong. This is so because under such circumstances the composer can give only a part of himself to his work; or, let us say, because he has to lay an essential part of himself aside for a moment. It is, of course, impossible to make rules in this regard; only the results are decisive. But past and present music alike furnish many an example of striking failure when a composer has temporarily stepped out of his chosen category—when a "popular" composer has tried his hand at "serious" music, when an essentially dramatic composer has tried to write orchestral or chamber music, or when a composer of symphonies has tried to write operettas.

This question of categories is important because I want to consider here the composer as such. I am not speaking primarily of any one category of music or of the standards or demands peculiar to it. I am not speaking of "serious" music, or "popular" music, or "instrumental" music, or "vocal" music, but of music and of the factors which go into its creation; of musical ideas and musical imagination; of "technique," "craftsmanship," and "style"; of "intelligence" and "instinct"; of the relation of the composer to his particular medium, and to his listeners. It is my firm belief that there is little difference in this respect either between composers who belong to different categories or between composers of different periods. There are great differences, certainly, in materials; there are differences in attitudes, as we all know. But these are historical or personal differences of style or character. In the course of many years during which I have met and talked with many composers, young and old, "serious" and "popular," good, bad, and indifferent, I have never noticed any appreciable difference between either their methods or their aims; and I believe that basically the aims of all composers have always been very much the same, however different the results. In any case, it is the similarities and not the differences which concern me here, and indeed these seem to me most important. Each composer has striven to bring to reality the music which is most truly music for him. The task of every composer is to give coherent shape to his musical ideas; or, as Artur Schnabel has so finely put it: "The process of artistic creation is always the same—from *inwardness* to *lucidity*."

What, then, is a musical idea? The term has acquired a somewhat stereotyped meaning, and curiously enough not because of over-precise usage but because of an unduly vague and loose one. True, one sometimes hears it used in a quasi-technical sense, as, for example, the "first idea" or the "second idea" of a sonata or a symphony. What is meant in this case: a motif, a phrase, or the whole group, often very complex, that forms one of the main contrasting elements in what we call the "sonata form"? Is it the equivalent of any of these terms, and if so, why is not the more precise term used? Is this word "idea" rather a term loosely adopted to indicate the small-scale changes in musical character or texture which may go into the making of a more complex rhythmic unit? If so, what is the criterion; what determines an "idea" as such, and where does it begin or end? I ask these questions because, in all simplicity, I do not know the answers to them.

43

On another level, we frequently read in a certain type of criticism that in this or that piece of music "the development is superior to the intrinsic worth of the idea," or something of the sort. But what on earth, we may ask, can such a statement mean? Is it not precisely through their development, actual or envisaged, that ideas reveal their worth, whether the ideas are of a musical or of some other type? How can development be in any real sense superior to the ideas developed? Or are we perhaps confronted simply with another of those quasi-plausible, important-sounding phrases which cloak more or less effectively either a basic lack of basic understanding or an inability to define exactly what bothers the critic?

I would say that a musical idea is simply that fragment of music which forms the composer's point of departure, either for a whole composition or for an episode or even a single aspect of a composition. I say "fragment" knowing full well that it can get me into difficulties. For in my experience, in which I include observation and analysis as well as composition, a "musical idea"—the starting point of a vital musical "train of thought"—can be virtually anything which strikes a composer's imagination. It may, certainly, be a motif, a small but rhythmically self-sufficient fragment of melody or of harmony; but I am fairly certain that by no means all motifs can be called "musical ideas." On the other hand, I could cite many examples where the most essential musical ideas, the elements that give the music its real character, consist not in motifs at all, but in chords, in sonorities, in rhythmic figures, or even in single notes of a particularly striking context. Sometimes—and this occurs, I think, more often though not always in works of composers of great maturity, in "late works," as we call them—one of the most important musical ideas, in a fundamental and motivating sense, may be not even a thematic fragment at all but some feature of the large design, such as a recurring relationship between two harmonies or keys, or even a linear relationship embodied in different aspects of the music at different moments.

Let me give a few examples, which will, of course, immediately illustrate the fact that the actual instance is more complicated than my somewhat schematic classification implies. Is not the famous "Tristan" chord (ex. 1a) a musical idea which, though it occurs most often in connection with a certain motif (ex. 1b),

(1a)

(1b)

does not occur by any means always in the same harmonic context? Or, in the Brahms Third Symphony, the motif at the beginning, F, A♭ F (ex. 2a) sets the

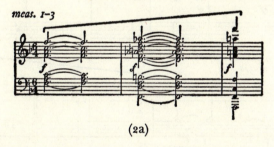

meas. 1–3

(2a)

stage for another, more deep-lying idea, the contrast between A natural and A♭ or F major and F minor which is implied in the harmonies of these measures, which appears in the famous clash between the outer

45

voices in measures three and four (ex. 2b), which deploys itself over a much larger area in the harmonic

meas. 3-5

(2b)

progression resulting in A major as the key of the second group (ex. 2c); and over a still larger area when

meas. 19-23

meas. 27-31

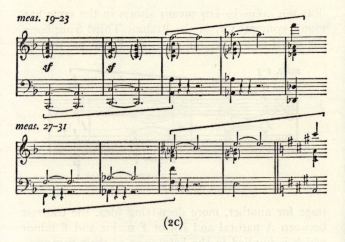

(2c)

F minor, leading to a final F major is chosen as the key of the Finale. In this case we have not only an example of a musical idea that, though absolutely auditory and not in any sense abstract in character, takes the form of a relationship playing an organic role in the music as a whole and helping to determine its largest outline. Though it is implicit in the motif with which the work begins, it is nevertheless independent of that motif and reaches far beyond it. Not only have we here an example of the idea itself, but we can see very clearly how it is developed, again in organic terms and not in the narrow sense of "development" as generally understood and taught in courses on "form."

Again, in the Scherzo of Beethoven's Quartet Op. 135, the notes F-G-A of the opening phrase (ex. 3a),

meas. 1–8

(3a)

are tremendously expanded to form the basis of the harmonic structure of the middle section, in which the keys F, G, A follow each other in direct succession (ex. 3b). Does this seem far-fetched? Then note how Beethoven takes us, from the extraordinary climatic passage in A, back to the original key, F, and the original phrase; first shifting the associations of the note A (ex. 3c), then anticipating the theme itself, but coming to a momentary pause on G, and then back to F (ex. 3d).

meas. 67-75

meas. 97-105

meas. 123-131

(3b)

meas. 185–193

(3c)

meas. 193–204

(3d)

Let me give a brief example from my own work. The first idea that came to me for my first Piano Sonata, begun in 1927, was in the form of a complex chord preceded by a sharp but heavy up beat (ex. 4a).

(4a)

This chord rang through my ear almost obsessively one day as I was walking in Pisa, Italy. The next day, or, in other words, when I sat down to work on the piece, I wrote the first phrase of the Allegro (ex. 4b);

meas. 27–32

(4b)

as you see, the chord had become simpler—a C minor triad, in fact, and its complex sonority had given way to a motif of very syncopated rhythmic character. Later it became clear to me that the motif must be preceded by an introduction, and the melody in B minor (ex. 4c), with which the Sonata begins, immediately suggested itself, quite without any conscious thought on my part. A few days later the original complex chord came back into my ear, again almost obsessively; I found myself continuing it in my mind (ex. 4d), and only then made the discovery that the

meas. *1-2*
Andante

(4c)

meas. 234-244
(*Allegro*)

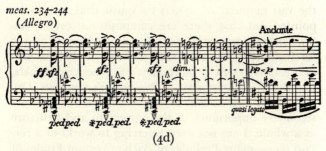

(4d)

two lower notes of the chord, F♯ and E, formed the minor seventh of the dominant of the key of B minor, and that the continuation I had been hearing led me back to B; that the germ of the key relationship on which the first two movements of the sonata were based were already implicit in the chordal idea with which the musical train of thought—which eventually took shape in the completed sonata—had started.

I point out these things in order to throw some light on some of the ways in which a composer's mind, his creative musical mind, that is, works; and more especially to illustrate the nature of the musical idea as I have defined it. Once more, I am not implying that the so-called principal "themes" of a given piece of music are not musical ideas or, in most cases, the most important formative ideas of the work. It is obvious that they frequently are. I have been trying to show, rather, that a composer's relation to his work is an organic one; that the conception and the composition of a piece of music are not a matter of set procedure, but a living process of growth. Above all, I have wanted to indicate that what we call "musical form" is, when it is real, as much a product of the composer's feeling and imagination as are the more obvious details or, let us say, the immediately striking and easily apprehended individual features such as the themes, the striking contrasts, and other matters with which the vast majority of writers on music deal. It may be pointed out that there are compositions, even sonatas, without, properly speaking, any "themes" at all; for instance, Mozart's sonata in F major, K. No. 332, or Beethoven's in F sharp, Op. 78. There are others, like the first movements of Beethoven's Quartets, Op. 74, or Op. 130, in which the themes are of obviously secondary importance to the movement and structure as a whole. I am not even referring to works of a certain type—many Preludes of Bach or certain Etudes of Chopin might be taken as examples—which are not thematic in any possible sense of the word, or in which the musical idea lies in what we may call pure structure. It might be worth noting also that these same works are so frequently and so obviously full of passionate expression: I mention this in order to emphasize that "structure" and "passion" are not in any sense mutually exclusive as is sometimes assumed, but that the one may, when the occasion demands, be the very essence of the other. I am also reminded of a story I heard once about Maurice Ravel and which I am quite sure is authentic. My informant asked him about the progress of the work which he was then composing, and he replied that he had it all finished except the themes!

The musical idea as I have described it is, then, the

element which gives the music its essential character, and I have also referred to it as "the starting point of a vital musical 'train of thought.'" The word "vital" is necessary because all composers, and possibly all musicians, have tones moving in their heads all the time, and thus often idly pursue musical trains of thought, as we all at times follow patterns of association which are not in any sense ideas at all. I was once asked to take part, along with some other composers, in a psychological experiment designed to test the supposed relationship of music to visual images of various kinds. We were given exact instructions as to timing and asked to jot down whatever fragments of music occurred to us as we looked at the images in question. I do not know what happened in the case of my colleagues; but in my own case the results showed very clearly that, though I had conscientiously tried to do what was demanded of me, I was actually, during the experiment, and all unconsciously, following a single musical train of thought. The fragments that came to mind at the respective "psychological moments" were all alike in meter, in tonality, and in general character; all of them could have been excerpts from the same composition. I did not feel, however, that the unwritten work of which they were a part was really good enough to finish. There was, in other words, no idea there—simply idle musical association which had not taken real shape.

I have used the expression "musical train of thought." I hope that some of my illustrations may indicate what I mean by this phrase and may serve at least as a helpful introduction to the descriptive remarks and instances that follow.

Actually a musical train of thought differs from any other train of thought only in the fact that its medium is tones, not words or images or symbols. The musical idea may, for instance, become clearer in shape and character, and become modified in the process, as Beethoven's sketchbooks so often show. A special fascination of his sketches is, indeed, the manner in which the various transformations of an idea always preserve and in fact progressively intensify the essential characteristics of the idea. It is impossible to give a general description of how this is brought about, but I should like to cite one example at least: the first phrase of the Finale, Allegro Appassionato, of the A Minor Quartet, Op. 132. An early version is in the key of D minor, since Beethoven thought at that time of using the theme in an instrumental Finale of the Ninth Symphony (ex. 5a). In the final

(5a)

version, one of the most wonderful phrases ever written (ex. 5b), the theme is utterly transformed. But note carefully what Beethoven has kept: (1) the motif of the first two measures; (2) the rise to the upper fifth in measure 4; (3) the harmonies C-G at the cadence, though these are in a more remote relationship to the key of A minor than to that of D minor; (4) the abrupt return to the tonic harmony, on the third beat of the eighth measure, anticipating the first beat of the next phrase.

Another example, likewise from Beethoven, is not easily illustrated. In an early sketch for the introduction to the last movement of the Hammerklavier Sonata, Beethoven has made brief and obviously rapid notes indicating the general character of the various short episodes that make up the whole passage, and in several cases where the musical line moves from a very

meas. *1-10*

(5b)

low note to a very important high one, he has simply indicated the note of departure and the note of destination, and connected the two with a "wavy line." In this way he has indicated in the most rapid fashion the general shape he had in mind. In the final version the early sketch is entirely recognizable, except for the fact that what I have described as the notes of destination have been changed, quite clearly to intensify the whole passage, and the episodes have been elaborated.

Before proceeding further I should like to make two observations on the general nature of what I have described as a musical train of thought. In the first place, though the phrase "train of thought" has the advantage of being familiar and therefore calling to mind familiar images, yet for strict accuracy it should be emphasized that a musical train of thought is in large measure actually a train of impulse or of feeling.

This is also true of many nonmusical trains of thought; the ideas or images are highly charged with emotion, and emotion frequently motivates the sequence of ideas. But in music it is the logic of sensation and impulse that determines the ultimate validity of the train of thought and gives the musical work not only its expressive power but whatever really organic unity it may possess. Every example given here clearly derives from a kind of dynamic momentum which is inherent in the musical ideas themselves, but which could not be deduced from them by any analytical process.

Secondly, the musical train of thought is both a conscious and a subconscious process. This, too, is not peculiar to music alone; in pointing it out I am perhaps calling attention to the obvious. Yet the relation of conscious and subconscious, of thought and impulse, of "mind" and "heart," if you like, in music, presents one of the least understood and certainly one of the most difficult of questions. It is one for which I can hope to find not any sweeping but at best only a piecemeal answer. I should like, however, to attack certain of its outlying phases.

For instance, there is the legend of the purely cerebral or, on the other hand, the purely impulsive composer. Both types are conceivable; and it is obvious enough that there is wide variation among composers and, perhaps especially, among individual works, as regards the relative preponderance of the conscious and the subconscious elements. This is true, of course, of personality itself. But—and I am speaking of general concepts, not of broad critical pronouncements to which we must accord a certain privilege of overstatement—it is clear, is it not, that a purely cerebral composer would be totally incapable of musical response, therefore incapable of being aware of musical relationships, therefore totally devoid of constructing recognizable musical patterns? I would be curious to hear, or even to see, his music, and curious, too, to know what impelled him to write it. Similarly, the purely instinctive composer would be one to whom all of the concepts which musical theory has down the ages so painstakingly constructed, in order to master the extremely raw material of sound and time—to whom all this would be essentially unknown. For even works of determinate pitch are the result of centuries of painstaking and highly conscious effort, of trial and error, as are also notes of fixed metrical value. Our awareness of them is the result of education, certainly not yet on a strictly formal level; but nevertheless, these basic premises of our musical culture are already the product of intellect or of consciousness operating on a very high level indeed, far above the level of anything we could conceivably call "instinct" as opposed to "thought."

Naturally, no one has ever really conceived of such interesting monstrosities as I have described. But in discussing them I have wished both to illustrate in as striking a manner as possible the coexistence of both the conscious and the subconscious elements, and also to suggest the impossibility of disentangling them. For not only is the individual composition the end result of a musical train of thought; in a larger sense the inner musical life of a single composer, and the composite musical development of a whole culture, represent also "trains of thought" on widely different scales. Not only do they present a picture of virtually impenetrable complexity, but they suggest an infinitely wide variety of possibilities, even of vital ones.

Two very convenient words may enable us not only to by-pass this fundamentally insoluble problem, but to envisage the relevant facts very clearly. I mean the words imagination and invention. Actually they mean very nearly the same thing: invention is the result, imagination the inner process. Both are the result of both conscious and subconscious processes and are subject to an extremely wide apparent range of variation in this respect. And while I doubt whether it would be possible to conceive of any very reliable standard of value in terms of the relative preponderance of conscious and subconscious elements, it is, I think, true that the latter—the subconscious—are the vitalizing ones. The deeper the composer's awareness of the basic elements of music, the more vital his imagination is likely to be. Nevertheless, the greater musical imaginations—the Bachs, the Mozarts, the Beethovens—have been those with not only the greatest impulsive power, but also the greatest intellectual mastery.

The role of the conscious, moreover, varies at different stages of the composer's development. It is likely to prove disastrous, for instance, for the young or inexperienced composer to become self-conscious at too early a stage: he is all too likely to find himself in the role of a critic before the fact, and to force his ideas into a preconceived pattern that may or may not be appropriate to them; and is likely as a result to tend to develop his resources in a one-sided and limited manner, at the risk of exhausting them through repetition.

The mature composer, on the other hand, will find himself inevitably, and as the natural result of his experiences, both forming general ideas and acquiring the ability to conceive his musical ideas in almost abstract terms. He will have acquired the most acute awareness, not only of the nature of his resources, but of his personality and his aims, and also the greatest ease in embodying them in music. In other words, the realm of the conscious will be greatly extended because he will have become consciously aware of so much that previously remained below the surface.

This is a very critical point in an artist's development; for it is the point at which he is most likely either to lapse into self-imitation, or to strike out boldly into new territory, in terms of his personal tradition rather than that impersonal one which he himself has found ready from his background as his point of departure. Need I cite the examples of the so-called "late" Beethoven, or of the old Verdi?

Let me, however, return once more to the musical train of thought, both conscious and subconscious. As we have seen, it may first of all sharpen or clarify the musical idea. It may then extend it, and carry its impulse forward into a large pattern. It can do this either by letting the idea grow into phrases and periods, that is, into rhythmic patterns of larger scale; or a similar development may take place partly through the accretion of other ideas which associate themselves with it in the composer's mind and thus become integrated into his whole train of thought. The composer will also, at moments, find himself impelled to throw his ideas into relief by appropriate contrasts. The particular contrasts adopted will, by the mere fact of opposing clearly defined elements, contribute to a more highly organized unity. The elements throw each other into relief, and by the quality of that relief characterize each other and make their individual contribution to the more complex character of the whole. This is on the assumption, of course, that the composer is a master in the sense of being able to achieve genuinely convincing results.

I am not going to speak in detail of composition, or of what is generally called by the somewhat unsatisfactory term "musical form." But I should like to indicate what I consider some of its underlying principles. These are very general, and the problem should be first of all envisaged as a general one. Tradition has consecrated the so-called "classic forms"—

minuet, rondo, sonata, and variation—and, I fear, raised them a little to the status of superstitions! Actually, it is not hard to demonstrate, through reference to fundamental principles, that there are very few basic patterns possible, but that these are infinitely various in application.

The first principle, perhaps, is the one called progression, or cumulation. Since music is an art of time and not of space, its effect must be cumulative and not static. Successive impressions must either maintain the level of intensity, of interest, of movement established at the outset, or they must raise it. Otherwise, in somewhat primitive terms, the tension relaxes, the ear becomes bored, and the music lags. I do not mean here the dynamic curve of a piece of music, the element of climactic tension and relaxation. This is only one phase of the principle of which I have been speaking and which I can define only in the most general terms. For each facet of the music—meter, pitch, texture, harmonic structure, sonorous quality—has its individual principles in this regard.

The second principle is association, or, in a much narrower sense, repetition. It serves two distinct purposes. First, through association musical ideas achieve their impact and drive home the precise significance the composer wishes to give them in the mind of the hearer. A musical motif, or even a phrase, means nothing in itself. This may sound startling, but a little thought will help to make it clear. The single musical impulse is too short, and too isolated; it is a gesture in the void which has not acquired substance. Only through association can it really become effective. This association may be of two kinds:

The music may be brought into association with words or dramatic gestures, and these elements will give it meaning. Though vocal music has tended to take over the principles of closely knit, purely musical association evolved through the development of instrumental music, nevertheless close association with the meaning of a text is often sufficient as a binding force, and may furnish the essential element of coherence even if other associations are absent.

Where there is nothing of a not strictly musical nature to contribute this element of association, it must be supplied from within the music itself. The music must, to state it cautiously, supply some element of repetition. The repetition need not be literal or complete, but it must be really associative in effect. I am not going to try to define what kind or degree of repetition will actually produce this desired associative effect; I doubt in fact whether it can be defined with any precision, since it is a psychological question and depends for its answer on the intentions of the composer in a given context. Literal-mindedness is clearly out of place here, though unfortunately it is not entirely unknown either among composers or among those who listen to music. A mere repetition of notes is not sufficient to create association; the internal gesture has to be present in some form. An inkling of what this signifies can be had by comparing the opening measures of the Eroica Symphony (ex. 6a) with

(6a)

the opening of Mozart's youthful overture to "Bastien et Bastienne" (ex. 6b) or with one of the leit-motifs of Salome's Dance (ex. 6c). The notes are similar, and in one case the rhythm is also; but the passages, in an inner sense, have no relationship to each other.

(6b)

(6c)

But when Beethoven leads us from the final cadence of the exposition to the beginning of the development section, the rhythmic pattern, even a very simple one, suffices (ex. 6d), and it can even be broken up so that

(6d)

it displaces accents without losing its associative power in this particular context (ex. 6e).

The principle of association thus gives significance to musical ideas and unity to musical forms. There remains the principle of contrast, which I have already mentioned and to which I need merely allude briefly at this point. As I have said, contrast throws ideas into relief, and thus determines as well as underlines their specific character. Here I will make only two further observations. First, it will be found generally true, and, I believe, almost a psychological law, that the various elements in a work must be so organ-

meas. *154-166*

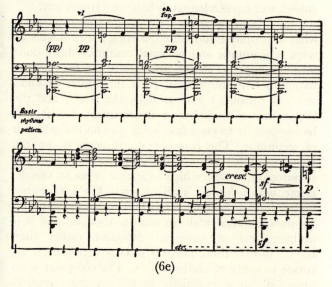

(6e)

ized that there is only one major and dominating contrast in the work when viewed as a whole, and only
one at any given moment. That is, on the largest scale
only two basic forces can be brought into opposition;
and if three or more elements are present, they must
be so organized as to present themselves in two main
groups. It would take too long to elaborate this principle, and it is enough here simply to state it as one of
the principles that the composer must discover in his
work of organization.

Secondly, the principle which I have called progression will extend itself to the various elements that are
brought into contrast. Just as a level of intensity must
be maintained and kept under control, so the level of
contrast, which is one of the major aspects of what I
have called the level of intensity, must be maintained.
A weak contrast, no matter what the context and its

63

character, or the proportion of the other elements involved, will never adequately balance a strong one.

I have been speaking here of the composer somewhat as a unique individual, solving his problems always in a unique and personal manner. I have done
this, as I hope is evident, because I think his essential
nature is best illuminated from that point of view,
and not because I wish to deny the reality and the
importance of tradition or environment. But it may
be worthwhile to say a few words also on the question
of technique. The composer's technique is, on the
lowest level, his mastery of the musical language, the
resourcefulness with which he is able to use its various
elements to achieve his artistic ends. On a somewhat
higher level it becomes something more than this; it
becomes identical with his musical thought, and it is
problematical in terms of substance rather than
merely of execution. On this level it is no longer accurate to speak of craftsmanship. The composer is no
longer simply a craftsman; he has become a musical
thinker, a creator of values—values which are primarily aesthetic, hence psychological, but hence, as an
inevitable consequence, ultimately of the deepest
human importance. At its very roots, as we have seen,
music embodies attitudes at least in their casual and
impulsive sense. On the highest level, through the
constructive sense of the composer, which brings musical impulses to their highest degree of organization,
it embodies basic human attitudes. This fact is deeply
involved in the musical problems of today, even on
the technical level, and cannot be separated from
them. Before considering them, however, we must
give some attention to the subject of music as it takes
its most actual and corporeal form. We shall deal next
therefore with the performer and his problems.

IV

The Performer

THE performer's work is, of course, begun by the composer. The latter not only composes the music, i.e. he conceives a coherent and meaningful pattern of tones and rhythms, but he translates the music he has thus conceived into symbols which enable the performer to bring it into actual, i.e. physical, being.

I have taken some pains in the above sentence to state the simple facts as I see them, and as directly and as accurately as possible. But you can see, I am sure, what difficulties I, a practical musician, would face if you should seriously call into question the various terms I have used. To "conceive," to "translate," to "bring into being"—these terms have a pleasant, cultivated sound, but, if examined carefully, they are seen to be still imprecise. For like so many other words used in regard to music, even established technical terms, they are borrowed from quite other contexts. Their meaning is oblique and therefore easily susceptible to misunderstanding: the train of associations carried with them are not by any means all relevant and tend sometimes to create obscurity rather than clarity.

It is interesting to consider how many of our technical terms apply originally to things seen rather than things heard, or to space rather than time. We speak of musical "form," "shape," "contour," "architecture." We talk of "color," "texture," "time," and we speak in these connections of "brilliance," "transparence," "plasticity," or "darkness," "thickness," or "fluidity." Even our terms "high" and "low" to describe pitch are quite arbitrary, as is proven by the fact that the Greeks, for instance, used the terms in the inverse sense. I do not propose inventing new terms to apply strictly to music. That would be virtually impossible. But it is worthwhile every now and then to examine carefully the exact musical sense of these terms, since that is often obscured by the tendency to take such purely analogical terms in too literal a sense and to find implications in the words that simply do not apply to the musical facts. The word "form" or "architecture," for example, led to the once famous comparison of the sonata form with an arch, the exposition and the recapitulation being compared to the two supporting pillars and the development section to the arch proper. It is not to the comparison as such that one objects, or even to the fact that, on closer examination, these turn out not to be functional parallels at all: the exposition and recapitulation do not "support" the development section, nor do they hold it at an appropriate height off the ground. The real flaw in such a comparison is in the fact that what we call "form" in the realm of time has nothing whatever to do with, and is in no real way comparable to, "form" as we know it in the realm of space. The one is fluid, and its essence is fluidity; the other is static, and its primary requirement is stability.

It is this essential and inherent quality of music— its fluidity, the fact that it is an art, even the art par excellence, of time—that has inevitably produced the performer. In music each moment is fleeting; it passes and cannot be completely recaptured, even through mechanical reproduction, which after all is imperfect simply through the fact of being mechanical. This fact, and the conclusions to be drawn from it, might well be considered as a kind of text, or at least as the point of departure for serious discussion of the performer and his function.

The point which cannot be made too clear or understood too thoroughly is that music, just because it is an art in which time and movement are the basic elements, needs constant renewal. This principle is extremely difficult to formularize and is full of pitfalls; but it is none the less real for that reason. Perhaps we can understand it most clearly if we consider a certain inherent limitation of that most useful instrument, the gramophone. I need not dwell on the fact of its usefulness, nor expatiate on the incredible advantages won through its invention and development. Any musician could add to the list of those advantages; and we of the mid-twentieth century are acquainted enough with the ordinary facts of technology to take it for granted that purely technical limitations can either be ignored or overcome. We may be sure that machines will be constantly improved and that reproductions will be constantly perfected. But what will never be overcome are the diminishing returns inherent in mechanical reproduction as such. We can listen to a recording and derive a maximum of pleasure from it just as long as it remains to a degree unfamiliar. It ceases to have interest for us, however, the instant we become aware of the fact of literal repetition, of mechanical reproduction—when we know and can anticipate exactly how a given phrase is going to be modeled, exactly how long a given fermata is to be held, exactly what quality of accent or articulation, of acceleration or retard, will occur at a given moment. When the music ceases to be fresh for us in this sense, it ceases to be alive, and we can say in the most real sense that it ceases to be music.

I shall later consider briefly certain fairly widespread misconceptions that could be easily corrected on the basis of what I have just pointed out. At this point I want only to draw attention to these facts, as a kind of underlying postulate to be kept constantly in mind in regard to all matters concerning performance.

I have said "the composer translates the music he has thus conceived into symbols." The musical text is obviously the link between composer and performer and therefore deserves some attention at this point. By means of it the composer sets down as clearly as possible the substance of his musical thought in order to indicate to the performer as exactly as he can what is to be done to reproduce this thought in sound. To make this clear, composers have, during the last thousand years, evolved a system of notation which is in itself a remarkable cultural achievement. They have learned to convey to those capable of reading it the finest subleties of pitch, of rhythm, of tempo, articulation, etc., so that an accomplished performer can within the limits of his technique reproduce these things at sight, with a startlingly close approximation to what the composer has heard in his imagination.

Our notation was invented in principle during the Middle Ages, and has been refined and developed by succeeding generations as the need arose. It is of course for that very reason based on a diatonic premise, and is therefore in certain respects problematical today. These problems cannot be minimized, every composer is aware of them, and every successive generation the more so. Nevertheless, I propose to leave the technical question quite aside, and discuss certain other aspects of notation which are not only of general interest but of the utmost relevance to the task of the performer.

Composers have always, I believe, set down in scores everything they considered necessary for the per-

former's guidance; and the evolution of musical notation, the development of increasing subtlety, has been
the result not of an independent effort but of the development of music itself. Certainly this has been true
in recent history. If Bach, for instance, was sparing
in dynamic indications, this was only partly owing to
the fact that he himself was able to supervise the performance of his works and therefore could afford to
neglect such matters. Still less, certainly, is it the result, as has sometimes been assumed, of any taboo
against so-called expressive performance. One must assume that musicians of Bach's generation and before
were as sensitive to the expressive modeling of
phrases, to clear and discriminating stressing of accents, to the throwing of contrasts into relief, even to
subtle inflections in tempo, as musicians have always
been. In a similar sense it is impossible to conceive of
composers like Josquin des Près, Orlando di Lasso,
even Palestrina, urging their singers to suppress the
natural eloquence of vocal inflection in order to
achieve the complete neutrality of effect which is
sometimes even today demanded as requisite for the
performance of this music, and for which the composers of the Renaissance are sometimes held up as
models.

Yet why did they not indicate minute dynamic
changes and inflections of movement in their texts as
later composers learned to do? Was it, perhaps, because they simply had not thought of doing so, either
because, as I have pointed out in connection with
Bach, they were so frequently involved in the performances of their works and therefore inclined to rely on
something like a so-called "oral tradition" passed from
one musician to another? Or was it because the musical sense was at that time so fresh, so sure of its roots,
and so uncontaminated by various influences that

have in later ages tended to corrupt it, that it never occurred to these early composers that their interpreters could go astray?

I am not a music-historian, and though I am not unacquainted with various phases of music history, I shall not attempt to answer these questions from an historical point of view. Furthermore, I feel that the historical approach to all such matters is not likely to give us the real answer. We would do better to start with the fairly plausible premise that the best composers were serious and mature musicians who brought to their work the whole, and not merely a part, of their powers, and on that basis to try to see the situation as it appeared to them.

By this approach to the question we come, I think, to the following conclusions: First of all, composers of all times have demanded of performers whatever liveliness and eloquence the latter could give. They have not, however, attempted to indicate the intangible factors in performance, and being men of experience as well as common sense, they have known full well that these factors, which make all the difference, indeed, between a good performance and a bad one, cannot conceivably be indicated in any score.

What composers have always tried to indicate in the clearest possible manner are the essential contours of the music, and the means required of the performer in order to make these clear. Whatever tempo and dynamic indications the composer gives are those he considers quite necessary for this purpose. They are functional in intent and are included because the composer feels they are needed in order to lay bare the proportions, to underline the contrasts, and to clarify, through articulation and through various types and gradations of accent, the rhythmic outlines of his score. Their function is to illuminate the form of the work by throwing its outlines into sharper relief.

In the period ending with Bach, the range of modulation was narrow, being restricted practically to six keys: namely, those corresponding to the consonant triads of the diatonic scale. Musical form consisted—in a general sense, be it understood—in the movement from one pivotal harmony to another, finally completing the circle back to the tonic. The various harmonies were pulled together either at the rhythmically important points—the various cadences—or, as in the fugue, by successive entries of the theme or subject, which from one point of view, at least, fulfilled exactly this purpose. That is, the subject was so constructed that by embodying the main harmonies of any given key it was capable of serving as the means by which each of these main harmonies of the fugue became crystallized in its turn. Strong contrasts such as characterized the music of later composers, with their symphonic and polythematic construction, were unknown to this music; and while, in the vocal music, details of an intensely expressive kind are frequently to be met with, the sense of these was made clear by their close association with the words of the text. Their sense was made so clear, in fact, that it is wholly impossible to believe that the performers did not show their awareness of them, through appropriate accentuation or otherwise.

Bach, frequently though by no means always, set off his contrasts by dynamic indications of the very simplest type: piano and forte, which always indicate generalized and large-scale contrasts. In the music of later composers, the sharper the essential contrasts on which the music is built, the more carefully the composer indicates and emphasizes these contrasts by nuances of all kinds. The tendency to minute indication runs in the most striking parallel to the development of minute elaboration and sharp contrast in musical detail, and the nuances are in the score, as always, for the purpose of throwing the detail into more drastic relief.

Any composer of the first magnitude may be cited in illustration of this fact. Possibly Beethoven's scores offer as good an illustration as any, since Beethoven stands as it were on the peak dividing the eighteenth and the nineteenth centuries and certainly partakes of both. His vast musical designs are not only completely integrated but, far more than those of any composer before him, they are extraordinarily rich in contrast and detail. It is for this reason that he carried the use of so-called expressive nuance so far, and what is amazing, and in itself worth years of study, is the absolute mastery—of one piece with his mastery of the design as a whole, and in fact one aspect of it—with which, by means of the nuances, he illuminates every essential detail of the whole and always in relation to this whole, that is, to the largest line.

To speak of dynamic and rhythmic nuances in this connection as "functional" is not to deny that they are essentially expressive. My intention is rather to demonstrate—what is certainly obvious to all mature musicians—that the expression, or expressivo, or expressivity, is in the music itself from the beginning and is not imposed from without. To perform a piece of music correctly, one plays not only the notes; one plays, in the first place, not so much notes as motifs, phrases, periods, sections, the rhythmic groups or, as I meant to imply in Chapter I, the impulses of which the music is composed. One sets them in the relationship to each other which the composer has indicated. And I firmly believe that a certain type of instrumental instruction which teaches students first to learn notes and then, as it is quaintly put, to "put in the expression," is not only musically but instrumentally false. But what is "expressivo" if not the accentuating of contrasts, the throwing of contours into relief? In the music of Beethoven and those who came after him— in fact one may eventually say in all the music of the tonal and post-tonal period—the expressivo is in the music itself and nowhere else. It is in the structure of the music and in the last analysis is identical with this structure. If for reasons of space I have omitted mention of the composers who came after Beethoven, this is none the less true of them also; and inevitably so. For it requires only a very little thought to see that, were it otherwise, the music would be inorganic, shapeless, and therefore inexpressive.

With these facts in mind we are in a better position to understand the relation of the performer to the composer. We understand, that is, what it is that the composer writes and therefore what it is that is to be performed. The composer indicates in his score the essentials of what for want of a better term we may call his musical thought; he indicates how the outlines, the profile of the music, as he has conceived it, can best be made clear; and these outlines, correctly understood, embody the musical movement, the musical gesture both in the large and in detail.

What, then, is the task of the performer? Is it simply fidelity to the composer's text, or is the performer himself a creative artist for whom the music performed is simply a vehicle for the expression of his personality?

Stated thus, the most obvious comment is that it is not "simply" either one of these things, or, in fact, simply anything at all. In what consists "fidelity" to the text? What constitutes "personality"? Let us acknowledge at the outset that fidelity is—fidelity, or truth; infidelity is falsehood. Are we to be understood, then, as asking whether or not the performer shall give a true or a false performance of the music? For after all, if the performer plays, let us say, a crescendo where a diminuendo is indicated, he is playing as surely falsely as he would be should he sound F# where the composer has asked for G.

What makes both of the above questions absurd is the word *simply*. For in the first place, fidelity to the composer's text is anything but simple, since the text itself is already very complex. It is complex because the composer has attempted to indicate (I can find no better word) by means of a vastly complex system of symbols the essentials of what I have called a musical gesture. And yet, as I have also tried to imply, a gesture, if it is to be living and genuinely expressive, must be unique; it must go beyond mere mechanical repetition and be invested with fresh energy if it is to live in time. Paradoxically enough, it cannot be really perpetuated in any other way; this is the very condition of its existence and, above all, of its endurance. For as I pointed out earlier, the listener—the person, who responds to the music, who re-creates it, either internally or externally—will respond to the musical gesture only as long as it strikes him freshly, or as long as he is capable of apprehending it as created anew and not as something mechanically repeated.

The agent of this re-creation is the imagination of the performer, or if you will, his "personality." It is his task, and I believe his whole task, to apply his imagination to discovering the musical gestures inherent in the composer's text, and then to reproducing them according to his own lights; that is, with fullest participation on his own part. This is only another way of saying that, having discovered as well as he can the composer's intentions, he must then apply himself to the task of reproducing them with the utmost conviction. It seems to me clear and beyond all doubt that both elements—fidelity, not so much to the text as to the music as expressed in the text, and conviction as animated by the musical nature of the performer—are essential. Without fidelity a performance is false, without conviction it is lifeless; in other words, it is hardly music.

Let us briefly investigate the two elements in turn. How, first of all, shall the performer discover the composer's intentions? As in so many questions having to do with music, the answer is simple, the process less so! The answer is, of course: by finding out what the composer has written. Here our difficulties begin, for I do not mean what he has written in terms simply of notes. The performer must first understand the music in terms of its articulation, its contours, and its proportions; he must discover, for instance, whether in a given case the composer has written a simple eight-measure phrase or, say, two four-measure phrases; whether an accent is a rising, falling, or climactic accent; whether the bar-line is to be ignored in the interests of the larger aspects of the rhythm, or whether the intention is rather to oppose a regular metrical accent to an expressive rhythmic displacement. He must be aware of the melodic and harmonic values as well as the associative similarities which characterize the context itself.

Shall I give examples? I once read a bit of criticism which struck me as one of the best I had ever seen, in spite of the fact that I had not heard the performance reviewed and therefore had no means of judging whether or not the critic was right. The critic spoke of a performance of Mozart's G Minor Symphony in which the conductor, he said, had performed certain sharply dissonant intervals in the last movement "as if he were not aware that they were there." Or, again: As a very young student, I for years nourished a dislike for the C Minor Piano Quartet of Brahms because I had misread an important melody as two short phrases. Had I been aware of the bass-line and of the harmonic progressions, which I knew, but to which, through inexperience, I had not paid sufficient attention, I would have realized it was a single eight-measure phrase; I would have realized that a certain disturbing sequential repetition was only an incident in a larger design instead of, as it seemed, a rather mechanical and perfunctory lapse of energy on Brahms' part.

I believe, in other words—and I must confess that my view is considered by many musicians as problematical—that the key to the music is to an overwhelming degree in the music itself, and not in any respect to associations that may have gathered around it, whether associations of so-called "tradition," of so-called "style," or those furnished by historical research. Tradition is one thing in the case of living composers or those only recently dead. The performer may easily find his imagination stirred by the memories of those who have heard the composer perform, or who have heard performances personally supervised by him; and here, too, gramophone records are of great assistance. But too often tradition is a somewhat spurious affair, as is illustrated by a note in a French edition of Bach, where a measure notoriously added to Bach's text by a nineteenth century editor was characterized as "mesure pas authentique, mais consacrée par la tradition"! Actually, tradition all too often "consecrates" distortions; it creates chains of distortions arising in the first instance only from the personal interpretations of distinguished performers and by the exaggerations of later ones. The custom which prevailed in my student days of always beginning Beethoven's Fifth Symphony with a pompous retarding of the famous four notes stemmed, I believe, originally from Hans von Bülow, who was certainly a great conductor, and who was perhaps influenced by Beethoven's remark, possibly facetious, about fate: "Da pocht das Schicksal an die Pforte." Nevertheless, the words "allegro con brio" stand on the score directly above the measures in question; and, at least to our contemporary taste, an enormous part of the power of this unique piece is derived from the cumulative effect of the relentless and unslackening movement with which it proceeds from the first note to the last, interrupted only by an occasional fermata.

Even more questionable, in my opinion, is an historical approach to such matters. It is based, in the first place, on purely documentary evidence; and though the documents may be, and generally are, of great interest, their interpretation is at the very best problematical. What did they actually represent, against the background of their time? What was the composer's relation to them? What, in fact, do the actual words mean in terms of the practice which was prevalent at the time that they were written? Are they to be taken literally, as rules, or rather as general guiding principles, which still allowed the performer a certain latitude? Finally, there is a danger in looking back at the past, which was itself moving forward to meet us: we tend, as we view it, instinctively to arrest it momentarily in its process of development and to treat it as if it were static, and hence, by implication, dead. This is the fallacy, in part, of those who insist on reproducing as far as possible the conditions under which music was performed in its time. It is at least a question whether those who insist that Bach should be performed on the harpsichord or the clavichord, are doing as he himself would have wished. There is some possible evidence that he was aware of the limitations inherent in both of these instruments and anxious to overcome them; and in any case our relationship to them is a quite different one from his. For him they were commonplaces—simply the means he had available, and the best means he had at his disposal, and not half-exotic variants, as they are to us.

In any case, we must decide whether we want music for the direct experience it can yield to us, or for the contribution it can make to fields of experience essentially outside it. Are we interested primarily in its message—forgive the hackneyed term!—for us, or in imagining how it sounded to its contemporaries? Certainly there will be those who feel that I am here on exceedingly dangerous ground, and that many an artistic crime has been justified in approximately the terms I have used. But in art, to tell the truth, all ground is very dangerous, and the most dangerous of all is that which would offer us fairly easy pseudo-criteria—which have nothing to do with our primary artistic impulses but which are, as it were, adventitious accretions to these—instead of the real but more difficult ones springing from the basic experiences of which music in essence consists.

The performer, then, must discover according to his abilities the composer's intentions and project them according to his own conviction. His insight into the music should deter him from the artistic crimes of which I have just spoken, and our insight should enable us to discover these, as well as others, when they are actually committed.

If we say that the performer must have insight into the composer's intentions, and insist on his obligation to familiarize himself with these, in what does his personal contribution consist? Is he merely a medium for transmitting these intentions more or less well, according to his technical capacities and his skill in deciphering the text?

I think that it should be clear that the performer is far more than this. First of all, musical notation, despite all efforts on the composer's part to translate his wishes and intentions, can never be exact. In projecting the work, the performer has to exercise individual judgment at many points; a performance is a specific occasion and subject to specific conditions. If he is concerned at all with the impact the work is to make, he will be aware of these conditions and be affected by them. He will arrange his program so that each work is thrown into the most favorable possible relief. I will not try here to elaborate on the question of program-making or to establish principles in regard to it; space does not permit, and I do not know whether it would be possible. It is, however, a matter which requires the performer's best efforts, and in which his musical insight must be brought fully into play, as must his intentions with respect to the occasion as such. He will be guided by his sense of appropriate contrast, by his sense of the demands which various works make on the listening powers of the hearers, and the type of adjustment that the transition from one piece to the next will require of them. For this, already, he needs his resources of sensibility and imagination as well as musical insight.

Secondly, the composer's text contains not only elements that must be considered as virtually invariable —pitch, relative note values, or the details of rhythmic articulation—but others that even under the strictest interpretation must be considered as variable according to the specific conditions under which the music is performed. To this category belong not only dynamic indications, and such intangible but vital questions as the sharpness with which the larger rhythmic articulations are to be "brought out," or their timing and spacing—what we might call the "breathing" of music, the fraction of space which must occur between phrases or periods or sections if the listener is to gain the appropriate sense of movement.

Special mention must be made, in this connection, of tempo, since it is a matter all too frequently misunderstood and, in fact, a favorite plaything of the snobs. The composer generally makes known the tempo he desires, often by precise metronomic indications, but musicians have always warned against taking these in a rigid and absolute sense. Actually tempo is subject to a number of conditions, some of which are obvious: a large instrument in a small room demands a slower tempo than a small instrument in a large hall. Inexperienced string players or young and untrained singers cannot sustain a slow tempo as can older, well-trained, experienced performers; and there are wide individual variations in this respect. There are also more subtle differences having to do not only with particular conditions of performance, but with the performer's individual characteristics—his "personality," if you like. And indeed we are speaking of personality in the profound sense.

I trust I will not be understood here as implying an endorsement of, or interest in, either the technical display or the aggressively "personal" interpretation which we associate with the pure virtuoso type. Some music demands both of these things and is written expressly for such exploitation. This music, however, is not under discussion here; it is eminently unproblematical and can hardly be said to need or to deserve extended comment. What I have in mind is the simple fact that if music consists in movement, or what I have called inner gesture, it is the performer who supplies the impulse and the energy through which the movement and gesture as conceived in the composer's imagination is given concrete form. This impulse and energy will come inevitably through him and will inevitably gain their particular character through his personality. The more truly he is able, in these terms, to engage himself completely in the music, to bring to it his own feeling for rhythm and movement, the more vital will be the performance. He will thus—provided, be it understood, that he really remains faithful to the composer's directions—embody in his performance at least some of the aspects of the piece and bring them to life. It is true that composers on occasion quarrel with this view, and insist upon what I would call a literal-minded rather than a genuinely spontaneous performance. My experience has been that when they do, the effect is almost certainly disastrous. For when the performer is not left free to follow the dictates of his own musical impulse and to achieve the eloquence natural to him, he becomes, with the best will in the world, constrained and unable to achieve any eloquence whatever. His performance fails to convince because there is no conviction behind it.

One must therefore accustom oneself to the fact that the performance of music is not an entirely simple affair. It is the result of a collaboration between the composer and a particular performer on a particular occasion. This is true also when the composer himself performs; the occasion is just as specific and the problems are similar. The composer is as unlikely as anyone else to play his work twice in the same way, and the more able the performance—the more eloquent and convincing, that is—the truer this is likely to be. The composer, too, must be faithful to the composition; he must in fact, and presumably will, learn to be. But he, too, will present one aspect of the work, and only one of various possible aspects.

This brings me back approximately to my starting place. Music is by its very nature subject to constant renewal, and the performer is not in any sense either a mere convenience or a necessary evil. By the same token, the idea of the "ideal" or even in any strict sense the "authoritative" performance is an illusory one. The music is not totally present, the idea of the composer is not fully expressed, in any single performance, actual or even conceivable, but rather in the sum of all possible performances. But having admitted this, we are bound to insist also that the number of possible performances is limited by the composer's text and by the musical intentions which that text embodies. Performers of genius, even with the best of intentions, sometimes overstep those limits, and apart from them we hear many "impossible" performances —impossible sometimes through distortion of the composer's idea, but sometimes also through lack of the vitalizing energy of a genuine impulse.

We may say also that precisely the greatest music is the most many-sided. It is capable of presenting different aspects to different generations and of retaining its vitality through all the different interpretations which these generations give to it. It contains within itself infinitely varied and even apparently contradictory phases, yet achieves the effect of not only the greatest vitality but the most complete consistency in each. Is it not this intense vitality, on a deeper level than all possible so-called interpretations, which really constitutes its greatness?

V

The Listener

WE ARE all very much concerned, these days, with the listener—the person who neither makes music nor performs it, but simply listens to it. The market is flooded with books of all sorts, fulfilling all sorts of functions for all sorts of listeners, from the child to "the man who enjoys *Hamlet*" and even "the intelligent listener"—analyses to edify him, critical chit-chat to flatter him, and gossip to amuse him. We have grade school, high school, and university courses designed to inform him and, if possible, to educate him in "appreciation," in "intelligent listening," and even "creative listening." On the radio he may find quiz programs, interviews with personalities, broadcast orchestra rehearsals, and spoken program notes, which have been known on occasion to be so long that there is not enough time for the broadcast of the music. Surely we are leaving no stone unturned in the effort to prepare the listener fully for the strenuous task of listening to music.

This is actually a peculiar state of affairs. Music, and in fact art in general, is not one of the so-called necessities of life, nor does it yield us any of the creature comforts associated with the standard of living of which we are so proud. Why then should we be so concerned about the listener? Is not music available to him, if he wants it? Should we not rather demand simply that the listener be given the best products available? Should we not rather concern ourselves with the quality of our music, and with ways of producing the highest quality, with providing the best possible education for our young musicians, and with creating opportunities for them to function according to their merits? In truth, should we not rather devote ourselves to improving the quality of our music, and to seeing that music of the highest quality is available for all that wish to hear it?

Of course, we have no such choice of alternatives; and the concern that is felt for the listener today is no chance development but the result of the situation in which music finds itself in our contemporary world. Possibly still more than this it is the result of these conditions as they have developed in the United States. In saying that it is "a peculiar state of affairs" I certainly do not wish to imply that it is one to be, if possible, abolished or even, in any fundamental sense, corrected. It is rather a phenomenon to be noted and one which, I think, must be thoroughly understood if our culture is to achieve, as we all wish, a healthy growth. It is not a condition in any basic respect characteristic only of our musical or even our artistic life; it lies at the very core of the situation created by technology and all of its various ramifications; by repercussions, that is, of technology upon the economic, the political, the social and therefore upon the whole cultural world. This situation is a fact to be dealt with, intelligently, let us hope. And while we may smile at some of its manifestations and raise our eyebrows at others, we will certainly be wasting both time and energy if we spend them deploring it. We should also be pursuing cultural mirages if we either ignored it or remained unaware of the questions it poses.

The point is that we are trying with all our means to increase the number of listeners to music, and that not just because we believe culture to be a good thing which should be made available to all members of a democratic society, though we believe this too, of course. It is a part of our tradition, and we have been at pains to educate ourselves. We have even covered a great deal of ground very rapidly; and though we sometimes let ourselves be unduly impressed by mere statistics which mean actually less than we think they do, there is nevertheless a residue of quite genuine achievement not to be gainsaid.

But the condition I have been speaking of—that is, our preoccupation with the listener, and our solicitude for his problems—has quite other causes. The crucial fact is that within a space of approximately twenty-five years the musical public has grown in size from some thousands, mostly in the larger centers, to a so-called "mass audience" numbering many millions. The development of the radio, plus the expansion of the gramophone business, more than any other factors, have brought this about and have undoubtedly played a major role in stimulating interest, not only in concerts and operatic performances, but in musical activity of all sorts.

Thus a far greater quantity of music must be furnished, for so large a public, than was ever dreamed of before. I am of course speaking of performances rather than compositions, and am taking into account the facts both of recorded broadcasts and the nation-wide broadcasts of the large networks. The point is that both the entrepreneurs and the musicians, those who purvey and those who produce, become thus necessarily involved in business enterprise on a large scale. Even before the radio and the gramophone had begun to play the decisive part they do in our musical economy today, various factors, economic and otherwise, had already greatly restricted the role of private patronage in our public musical life. The purveyors of music, however disinterested, found themselves obliged to count costs and to concern themselves with profits. I say "however disinterested," and indeed I feel that in order to understand the situation as it has developed it is necessary to assume this disinterestedness. For the situation I am describing has not been made by individuals at all. It is the result of economic facts the like of which have never existed before; and the facts in question are far too large in scope, too intricately interwoven with the very bases of contemporary life, to be influenced one way or the other by the decisions of individuals.

When music or any other product is furnished to millions of individuals, it is bound to become necessary to consider the tastes of those individuals in relation to the product offered them. Those who furnish the product are obliged to produce as efficiently and as cheaply as possible the goods which they can sell to the most people; they are obliged, furthermore, to try to persuade the people to whom they sell that it is preferable to buy the goods that are most cheaply produced; it is furthermore necessary to do everything possible to enhance the value of the goods sold. If they fail to do these things they are taking foolish economic risks. The larger the quantities involved, the greater the potential profits; but while this is true, it is also true that the risks of possible catastrophic loss are greater. These facts are elementary; not only do they apply vitally to the situation of music today, but I believe that an understanding of them is absolutely indispensable if we are to understand any economic, political, or social aspects whatever of the contemporary world.

In brief, the "listener" has become, in relation to these facts, the "consumer," and however unaware we as individuals are of this, it is nevertheless the basic explanation of our interest in him. Though neither he nor we have chosen this role for him, circumstances have made it inevitable. In relation to the same facts (and please note the phrase carefully, for I shall try to show later that these are not the only facts), the status of the artist in our society has undergone a remarkable change. He has become (in relation to the same facts) no longer a cultural citizen, one of the cultural assets of the community with purely cultural responsibilities, but what is sometimes called a cog in the economic machine. He is asked and even in a sense required to justify his existence as a plausible economic risk; to, as we say, "sell" himself as a possible source of economic profit. Then, having done so, he must produce what is required of him in this sense. He, too, has an interest in the listener; it is the listener who buys his wares and therefore justifies his continued existence as an efficient cog. He has to be constantly aware, in fact, of the requirements of the machinery in approximately the terms I have outlined above. For the aims of business are essentially short-range aims, and it is doubtful whether business, as such, can conceivably operate on any other basis. It can allow itself the luxury of the long-range view only to the extent that it builds up enormous surpluses which make risks economically possible, and even then only under circumstances offering reasonable hope of long-range rewards.

Let me say once again that I do not consider this the entire picture of our cultural situation or of our cultural prospects. I shall later try to show why I do not believe it to be so. Furthermore, these remarks are generalizations, and subject to elaboration, with intricate scoring and with many subtleties of nuance. I do not intend to score them for you here. But we cannot understand the listener unless we know who he is in terms of the conditions actually prevalent. We must see him, in other words, not as an abstraction but as an existing and concrete figure in our musical society.

But it is not mainly in his role of consumer that I

wish to speak of the listener. The question for us is rather his own experience of music—what hearing a understanding consist in, and, finally, what discri nation involves. What, in other words, is his relation ship to music? How can he get the most from it? How can music mean the most to him? In what does his real education consist? Finally, how can he exercise his powers of discrimination in such a way as to promote valid musical experience in others and, so to speak, in the world in general?

I think we can distinguish four stages in the listener's development. First, he must hear; I have already indicated what I mean by this. It is not simply being present when music is performed, nor is it even simply recognizing bits of the music—leit-motifs, or themes, or salient features in a score. It is rather, as it were, opening one's ears to the sounds as they succeed each other, discovering whatever point of contact one can find, and in fact following the music as well as one can in its continuity. We perhaps tend to ignore the fact that listeners are, like composers and performers, variously endowed, and also that they differ very widely in experience. But this initial stage in listening to music is an entirely direct one; the listener brings to the music whatever he can bring, with no other preoccupation than that of hearing. This is of course what is to be desired; it is the condition of his really hearing. He will hear the music only to the extent that he identifies himself with it, establishing a fresh and essentially naïve contact with it, without preconceived ideas and without strained effort.

The second stage is that of enjoyment, or shall we say the primary response. It is perhaps hardly discernible as a "second stage" at all: the listener's reaction is immediate and seems in a sense identical with the act of hearing. Undoubtedly this is what many listeners expect. And yet, on occasion, one may listen to music attentively, without any conscious response to it until afterwards; one's very attention may be so absorbed that a vivid sense of the sound is retained but a sense of communication is experienced only later. It is this sense of communication to which I refer under the term "enjoyment"; obviously, one may not and often does not, in any real sense, "enjoy" what is being communicated. There is certainly some music that we never "enjoy"; experience inevitably fosters discrimination, and there is certainly some truth even in the frequent, seemingly paradoxical, statement that "the more one loves music, the less music one loves." The statement is true in a sense if we understand it as applying to the experience of the individual, and not as a general rule. But if our relation to music is a healthy one—that is to say, a direct and a simple one—our primary and quite spontaneous effort will be to enjoy it. If this effort becomes inhibited it will be by reason of experience and the associations that inevitably follow in its train. We shall in that case have acquired a sense of musical values, and our specific response will be curtailed in deference to the more general response which our musical experience has given us.

The third of the four phases I have spoken of consists in what we call "musical understanding." I must confess that I am not altogether pleased with this term. To speak quite personally if not too seriously, a composer will certainly have every right to feel pleased, but he may not feel entirely flattered, when he is told "I love your music, but of course I have no right to an opinion—I don't really understand it." In what does "musical understanding" consist? The difficulty, I think, comes from the fact that while, as I tried to show in the first chapter, the instinctive bases of music, the impulses which constitute its raw materials, are essentially of the most primitive sort, yet the organization of these materials, the shaping of them into a means of communication and later into works of art, is, and historically speaking has been, a long and intricate process and one which has few obvious contacts with the world of ordinary experience. The technique of every art has, of course, its esoteric phrases; but in the case of visual art even these phases are relatively accessible to the layman, since he can, if he is really interested, grasp them in terms of quite ordinary practical activity. He will have learned early in his life to be aware of the basic facts of size, contour, color, and perspective on very much the same terms as are required for his perception of visual art. He can to a certain extent appreciate the artist's problems in these terms and can define his response, at least on an elementary level, in terms satisfactory to himself. This is even truer in the case of literary art, since he constantly uses words and to a greater or a lesser degree expresses himself by their means. Like Molière's "bourgeois gentlemen," he has talked in prose all his life. His feeling for the values of both visual and literary art consists therefore in a high degree of refinement, and an extension, of experiences which are thoroughly familiar to him, through analogies constantly furnished by his ordinary life.

In the case of music there are no such clear analogies. The technical facts which are commonplace to the composer, and even many of those proper to the performer, have no clear analogies in the ordinary experience of the non-musician. The latter finds them quite mysterious and, as I have already pointed out, tends to exaggerate both their uniqueness and their inaccessibility to the layman. And if the latter finds it difficult to conceive of the mere fact of inner hearing and auditory imagination, how much more difficult will he find such a conception as, for instance, tonality, or the musical facts on which the principles of what we call "musical form" are based. He is likely not only to regard music *per se* as a book in principle closed to him, but, through the impressive unfamiliarity of whatever technical jargon he chances to hear, to misunderstand both the nature and the role of musical technique. It is likely to seem to him something of an abstraction, with an existence of its own, to which the sensations and impressions he receives from music are only remotely related, as by-products. How often, for instance, have I been asked whether the study and mastery of music does not involve a knowledge of higher mathematics! The layman is only too likely to react in either one of two ways, or in a combination of both. He is likely, that is, either to regard music as something to which he is essentially a stranger, or else to regard its generally accepted values as arbitrary, pretentious, and academic, and both to give to it and to receive from it far less than his aptitudes warrant.

The surprising thing is that all of these conclusions are based on a mistaken idea as to the real meaning of musical "understanding." Technique is certainly useful, not to say indispensable, to the composer or the performer; a knowledge of musical theory is certainly an advantage to the performer and practically inescapable for the composer. But theory, in the sense of generalization, is not of the least use to the listener; in practice it is a veritable encumbrance if he allows preoccupation with it to interfere with his contact with the music as such. He can certainly derive both interest and help from whatever can be pointed out to him in connection with the specific content of a piece of music; but he will be only misled if he is persuaded to listen in an exploratory rather than a completely receptive spirit. Any effort to help him must be in the direction of liberating, not of conditioning, his ear; and the generalizations of which musical theory consists demonstrably often lead him to strained efforts which are a positive barrier to understanding. The "technique" of a piece of music is essentially the affair of the composer; it is largely even subconscious, and composers frequently are confronted by perfectly real technical facts, present in their music, of which they had no conscious inkling. And do we seriously believe that understanding of Shakespeare, or James Joyce, or William Faulkner has anything to do with the ability to parse the sentences and describe the functions of the various words in *Hamlet* or *Ulysses?*

Of course not. Understanding of music, as relevant for the listener, means the ability to receive its full message. In order to define it, to describe what it implies, I can only refer to a passage in Chapter I. In the primary sense, the listener's real and ultimate response to music consists not in merely hearing it, but in inwardly reproducing it, and his understanding of music consists in the ability to do this in his imagination. This point cannot be too strongly emphasized. The really "understanding" listener takes the music into his consciousness and remakes it actually or in his imagination, for his own uses. He whistles it on the street, or hums it at his work, or simply "thinks" it to himself. He may even represent it to his consciousness in a more concentrated form—as a condensed memory of sounds heard and felt, reproduced for his memory by a vivid sensation of what I may call character in sound, without specific details but in terms of sensations and impressions remembered.

It is for this reason that I am somewhat skeptical of the helpfulness of the kind of technical tid-bits and quasi-analyses sometimes offered to the listener as aids to understanding. The trouble with them, as so often presented, seems to me that the essential facts of musical technique cannot really be conveyed in this way. To give one instance, musicians talk, for convenience, about what we call the "sonata form." But they know, or should know, that the conception "sonata form" is a rough generalization and that in practice sonatas, at least those written by masters, are individual and that each work has its own form. To speak of "sonata form" without making clear what constitutes "form" in music, as such, is to falsify, not to illuminate. It is to imply that the composer adapts his ideas to a mold into which he then pours the music. It is also to lay far too much emphasis on what are called "themes," to the detriment of the musical flow in its entirety. What the layman needs is not to acquire facts but to cultivate senses: the sense of rhythm, of articulation, of contrast, of accent. He needs to be aware of the progression of the bass as well as the treble line; of a return to the principal or to a subsidiary key, of a far-flung tonal span. He needs to be aware of all these things as events which his ear witnesses and appreciates as a composition unfolds. Whether or not it is a help to have specific instances pointed out to him, it is certain in any case that his main source of understanding will be through hearing music in general, and specific works in particular, repeatedly, and making them his own through familiarity, through memory, and through inner re-elaboration.

I hardly need point out the fact that this is as true in regard to so-called "modern" music as it is to old. Where the music is radically unfamiliar the three processes I have described are slower. It must therefore be heard more often than the older music needs to be heard. At the beginning the impressions will be chaotic—much more chaotic than impressions produced by purely fortuitous sounds. The impression of chaos comes simply from the fact that the sounds and relationships are unfamiliar; their very consistency—since it, too, is based on contexts which are unfamiliar—seems like a denial of logic. As long as this impression prevails the listener has not yet made contact with the music. In connection with contemporary music, I have often observed the first sensations of real contact, while the musical language in question is still essentially unfamiliar but beginning to be intelligible. These first sensations may be acutely pleasurable; the work becomes highly exciting, conveying a kind of superficial excitement which disappears when the stage of real understanding is reached and gives way to an appreciation for the real "message" of the work. Once more, the key to the "understanding" of contemporary music lies in repeated hearing; one must hear it till the sounds are familiar, until one begins to notice false notes if they are played. One can make the effort to retain it in one's head, and one will always find that the accurate memory of sounds heard coincides with the understanding of them. In fact, the power to retain sounds by memory implies that they have been mastered. For the ear by its nature seeks out patterns and relationships, and it is only these patterns that we can remember and that make music significant for us.

The listener's final stage is that of discrimination. It is important that it should be the final stage since real discrimination is possible only with understanding; and both snobbery and immaturity at times foster prejudices which certainly differ from discrimination in any real sense. Actually it is almost impossible not to discriminate if we persist in and deepen our musical experience. We will learn to differentiate between lasting impressions and those which are fleeting, and between the musical experiences which give full satisfaction and those which only partly satisfy us. We will learn to differentiate between our impressions, too, in a qualitative sense. In this way, we cultivate a sense of values to which to refer our later judgment. We will learn that music is unequal in quality; we will possibly learn that instead of speaking of "immortality" in the case of some works and of the ephemeral quality of others, we must conceive of differences in the life span of works—that some works last in our esteem longer than others without necessarily lasting forever. We will learn finally to differentiate in the matter of character, to be aware of the differences between works in ways which have no relation to intrinsic worth. In other words, we will become critics.

The critic is, in fact, the listener who has become articulate, who has learned to put his judgments and his values into words. I am not, for the moment, speaking of him in his professional capacity but as what I may call the end-product of the listening process. It is important that we understand that he is the end-product, because otherwise we will, I think, understand correctly neither the listener nor the critic. I spoke earlier of the speed with which we, in the United States, have developed our culture and of the constant danger of producing a type of artistic culture in which the critic rather than the productive artist is the central figure. Lest this particular turn of phrase seem to indicate a prejudice against critics, which I do not feel, let me put it a little differently. The danger, and a very real one, is that we allow ourselves to cultivate, on the first level, a predominantly critical attitude toward art in precedence over a love for it; that in our overeagerness to produce what we consider mature results, we make of judgment an end in itself instead of the natural and full-grown by-product of a total artistic experience.

For as a growing culture, and possibly in regard to music more than anything else, we still have a strong residue of the diffidence and the self-distrust which results from the consciousness that we have not a thousand-year-old tradition behind us. In cultural matters we tend to question ourselves, our feelings, and our judgment, at every turn. This is, I believe, a deep-seated attitude, and one not always apparent on the surface of things. It expresses itself in a variety of attitudes, each of them potentially dangerous to our musical development, and still present in spite of the achievements of the past half-century. These achievements are real, even after we have dismissed all of the spurious claims resulting from the fact that we have money to buy goods produced elsewhere, and the fact that we often buy not wisely but too well, and that we possess not only the technique of salesmanship but a tremendous territory in which sales are possible. After we have looked beyond these claims and tried conscientiously to appraise the situation in an objective manner, our achievements are still impressive. But they will be in the last analysis sterile unless we overcome our tendency to self-questioning and learn to give ourselves freely to musical experience, and to recognize that mature artistic judgment can result only from the love of art; that any judgment in the absence of love is sterile and therefore false.

A healthy musical culture is one in which the creative function, the function arising from a strong and prevalent love for music, is the primary one, and in which the activities of the composer, the performer, and the listener (and in the category of listener I include the critic) are in their several ways embodiments of that love. It is obvious that real love for music, as for anything else, depends on inner security; but it is also true that inner security depends on the strength of love. What I have described as the critical attitude, the attitude which implies a forced or premature attempt to arrive at artistic judgment, is in reality only the result of basic insecurity; and there is some evidence that such insecurity threatens to become endemic to our culture. Are we not all familiar with the type of pseudo-sophistication that gives more importance to aversions than to preferences, that is more afraid of loving what is bad than of disliking what is good? Do we not all know too well the type of artistic talent which we see embodied in an essentially divided or imperfectly integrated personality—a personality which, like all mature personalities, contains both creative and critical elements, but in this instance divided through the fact that the two faculties are distrustful both of each other and of themselves? In such cases the creator-personality is inhibited through fears for the soundness of his artistic judgment, and the critic-personality is inhibited through fears that its mere existence may indicate a lack of creative force. Finally, there is always the danger that the young and gifted composer may be thrown into self-doubt, and his development seriously threatened, by excessive self-consciousness at exactly the moment when he should rightly be finding his own inner security, through the discovery of his own creative nature by means of constant and untroubled experimentation and productiveness.

The critic, then, finds his true function as an experienced listener, one who has made a vital contact with music and who has developed powers of discrimination through following up this contact to the point where he becomes conscious of values in a generalized sense. His importance in our total musical economy is obvious. I mean our musical economy, and not the economics of our musical life, where his professional role is considerable but more problematical in effect. For in accordance with his gifts he has the power to contribute strongly to musical life, through illumination of the real issues which are vital in any particular time and place. What these issues are for our contemporary world, I shall discuss more fully later. I wish to emphasize here simply that the true role of the critic is precisely to throw these issues into the clearest possible relief. His true role is that of collaborator, so to speak, in a common cultural effort in which composer and performer and listener all participate.

His role is, in a limited sense, a particularly crucial one, owing to our special history and the conditions under which music developed here. For many years, as it were, we imported all our music. It was a product of a tradition developed elsewhere, and our problem was to gain for ourselves the fruits of this tradition. The critic had the task of interpreting the tradition to the American public, and in consequence there was very little he could do except to take due note of judgments and values that had already reached maturity elsewhere. Today, with the ever-increasing development of a rich musical life of our own, he is forced to swim in more perilous waters and to discover values of his own. It is small wonder that he often shows a certain reluctance to do this, and takes refuge in writing long columns on the season's sixth performance of Tristan, or indulging, to cite a ghastly example I shall never forget, in vituperation of Critic B because the latter had written an unfavorable review of a book by Critic C, of whom Critic A (the author of the review in question) approved because he (Critic C) had written disparagingly of Critic D's book on Mozart. A veritable tangle of critics, with poor Mozart, in this case representing the only actual music involved in the whole matter, four steps away! All this is the result of an inherited habit of regarding music as a commodity to be bought and enjoyed, but in the production of which we have no part. I would like to suggest that this is not criticism at all; it is basically irrelevant chit-chat which can have no constructive consequence whatever. Because criticism, like composing, like performance, must spring out of a genuine culture; that is, a pervasive musical impulse, a living and shared relationship to music, which communicates itself within the framework of some kind of common experience. Our musical culture cannot exist, in fact, on any other terms; and the critic will properly fulfill his function only in energetic awareness of the issues and personalities immediate to the cultural situation in which he, too, lives and of which he, too, is inexorably a part. For even what we call the past is for us a part of our present experience, and our relationship to it is false unless we derive living experience from contact with it; and we cannot have that unless we are aware of ourselves and the forces that have gone into our own making. I am not suggesting that the critic should invariably praise contemporary music or even that he should necessarily ever do so. But it seems to me clear that his central task, as a critic, is to be aware of it and to understand it, and to become fully conscious of the issues that have brought it into being. These bring into play his real powers as a critic, make the greatest demands on his powers of discrimination and offer a truly exciting challenge to his gifts. They are certainly, as I have said, the most dangerous, and yet they are also the most stimulating, waters in which he is called upon to swim.

Finally, to conclude our discussion of the listener, let us ask what he demands of the composer. The question has been asked frequently in our time; it has been given tragic power in dictatorships where the effort has been made, sometimes as in Nazi Germany with ruthless force, to coordinate the artist to the purposes of those in power. Less ruthless, less consistently, and even less consciously applied, but none the less real, are the pressures which arise in such large-scale economy as I described at the beginning of this chapter —pressures such as those summarized for the theatrical world in the words "Broadway" or "Hollywood." The slogan, sometimes couched in more refined and even quasi-intellectual terms, is "Give the public what it wants"; but as I have pointed out, there is strong pressure on the public, too, to want what it is cheapest and most generally economical to give.

Let us phrase the question in more general terms: What does the listener demand from music? The answer will inevitably be that a variety of listeners want a variety of things. But on any level it may be taken for granted that the listener wants vital experience, whether of a deeply stirring, brilliantly stimulating, or simply entertaining type. If we understand this we should understand, too, that the composer can effectively furnish it only on his own terms. He can persuade others to love only what he loves himself, and can convince only by means of what fully convinces him. It is for this reason that the artist must be completely free, that such a question as I have stated here can ultimately have no importance to him. His obligation is to give the best he can give, wherever it may lead, and to do so without compromise and with complete conviction. This is in fact natural to him; if he is a genuine artist he cannot do otherwise. He can be sure that if he fully achieves his artistic goals, he will find listeners, and that if he has something genuine to say, the number of his listeners will increase, however slowly. This, in any case, will never be for him an artistic preoccupation, however much it may prove to be a practical one.

Composers, like poets, are born, not made; but once born, they have to grow. It is in this sense that a culture will, generally speaking, get the music that it demands. The question, once more, is what we demand of the composer. Do we demand always what is easiest, music that is primarily and invariably entertainment, or do we seriously want from him the best that he has to give? In the latter case, are we willing to come to meet him, to make whatever effort is demanded of us as listeners, in order to get from his music what it has to give us? Once more, it is for the listener and not for the composer, as an individual, that the answer is important. On the answer we ultimately give depends the future of music in the United States.

VI

Music in the World Today

AT VARIOUS times in this book I have referred to a fact which I consider very important as a premise to this final chapter. That fact is the essential unity of musical experience. It can be regarded from several angles. First of all, the composer, the performer, and the listener are in a certain sense collaborators in a total musical experience, to which each makes his individual contribution. Secondly, not only are the performer and the listener, in a real sense, re-experiencing and re-creating the musical thought of the composer, but they are, also in a real sense, adding to it. We might even say that, according to the various gifts involved, the three functions sometimes overlap, with the performer supplying whatever for him is missing in the work of the composer, the listener hearing the composition sometimes beyond the performer, and the composer, to a very important degree, visualizing (with his ears and not with his eyes, be it understood!) his work in terms of both performance and sounds heard. Finally, a given musical environment produces all of these phases if it is, as we might say, musically alive; if, that is, the love for music is a strong and vital factor in people's lives. In such an environment all these—composer, performer, and listener—are subject to similar influences, and hence may always be presumed to show somewhat similar trends. A similar musical spirit or musical mentality will operate through them all—all of them, that is, whose musical activities embody values that are new, and hence characteristic of that environment.

When we say "contemporary music," then, we refer not only to the music composed today, but to many other manifestations characteristic of our time and of what I might perhaps call the contemporary musical mentality. This "musical mentality" (it is more inclusive than what we might refer to as the "spirit of the times") refers not only to the music of Schönberg and Bartok, Stravinsky and Milhaud, Hindermith, Krenek, Prokofieff and Copland and Shostakovitch. It includes the performance of, for instance, Klemperer and Ansermet, of Schnabel and Casadesus, of Feuermann and Szigeti. It includes the fact that more works of Haydn and Mozart, of Berlioz and Verdi are performed more often today than they were twenty-five years ago; that we seldom hear, today, the Symphonic Poems of Liszt; that Wagner is certainly a darling of the Philistines, and Debussy a favorite of the multitude, whatever either may be for the rest of us. It includes, of course, the fact that some American composers have won national and even international reputations; it includes also such diverse phenomena as changed attitudes in musical education, the manner in which the conductor has become enthroned in the popular mind, the prevalence of interest in musicology, or the character of so-called "popular" music of today as compared with that of thirty-five years ago.

I shall not add to the list, nor am I going to attempt a definition of what I have called the "musical mentality" of today. Where, indeed, does "yesterday" end and "today" begin? What I do want to stress, first, is that real, extremely tangible changes have taken place in the last thirty-five years; that the inner as well as the outer complexion of music is something quite different today from what it was then. Secondly, our whole musical life, our whole musical outlook or point of view, and not alone the kind of music written, have changed. It is true that some of this change is, if one examines it closely, peripheral; and it is true that if we regard the greatest artistic personalities, those whose influence is most profound and sometimes even the most revolutionary, we are struck by how much, from one generation to another, they resemble each other. This is because they are inclusive and not exclusive personalities. Not only do they have deep roots in tradition which are never completely obscured, however far-flung the revolutionary impact, but their embrace is also of the widest: it contains many elements that would seem contradictory combined in lesser personalities, and it also reaches far beyond the limits set by fashion and by the prevailing taste of a particular moment. Hence it is often in the followers rather than in the leaders that we most clearly perceive the real character of a period, and it is in cumulative detail rather than in a few single dominating facts that we find the tangible evidence of that character. Looked at in this way, the change that has taken place within the space of one generation is striking indeed.

Finally, it is clear that this change has been brought about primarily by musicians. This is a point to which I want to return later, for it is of the utmost importance in connection not only with what we may call the sociology of music, but with all questions having to do with the relations between the artist and the public. I have not yet listed these questions among the earmarks of our period; but, as I have pointed out, they are questions that are particularly acute today. It is little more than banal to say that we live in a transitional period, but I want to discuss at some length the specifically musical aspects of this period of transition. It is of course apparent that the transitional character of the period is all-pervasive and that in fact what I have called its musical aspect is such a small part of the whole that it is often ignored, still more often misconceived, and frequently, even by those who understand it best, treated as an isolated development, quite without relation to the situation of mankind as a whole.

Yet one of the fascinations of history is the way that apparently self-sufficient currents of development coincide in a single historical movement. Different sets of facts, having no apparent connection with each other, seem over and over again to coincide in such a manner that it is tempting to seek, or perhaps to assume, connections and to find only specious reasons for them. Fundamental and far-reaching changes in one so-called "field" of human activity are likely to coincide with changes of an equally far-reaching character in many others. This is why we speak in broad historical terms of such concepts as, for example, the Middle Ages, the Renaissance, or the Romantic Movement— a well-known fact, on which there is no need to dwell. What is far too seldom pointed out, however, is that, at least in music, the inner logic, even the technical and, if you like, the esoteric structure of the special and apparently autonomous field, leads to the same "critical moment" to be observed in other fields of human activity, and furnishes an amply sufficient motivation for this critical moment. One result is that broad historical generalizations, even when they seem valid in general, are so often specious and vulnerable in detail; and their general validity is rendered at least suspect by reason of the fact that, in the absence of precise knowledge—knowledge of the inner growth of a specified art or a specified technique—generalizations are so often easily seen to be thoroughly specious. So, while each of the three phases of music mentioned above as examples taken at random is in the most obvious sense a phase of general culture, motivated by the logic of general events, each is also the culmination of a process of musical development which we can interpret in terms of music alone. The materials of music had been ripening, as it were, for this very moment, and the moment seems only the inevitable consequence of developments which had been taking place within the most self-contained musical sphere. These developments can be formulated, quite adequately, in terms of the musical ear alone, and it can be shown that those which are considered most generally in the widest, cultural sense, can be considered in an even more precise sense as purely musical developments—developments of our musical hearing, of the form the musical ear, as I described it in Chapter II, had acquired at that particular moment.

So, what of our own day? When we say that we are living in a transitional period we mean, I think, that fundamental changes are taking place, and that we are not yet entirely sure what the definite outlines of the future will be. That changes are taking place, in fact have already been carried far, there is no doubt. Musicians have been aware of this fact for many years, and if one wishes to measure the extent of the change, one only has to compare, not the so-called "advanced" music, but conservative, or even popular, music written today with that written thirty-five years ago. One finds immediately that what was then problematical, sometimes extremely so, has now become assimilated, and that much that is now taken for granted and considered quite harmless would have shocked the musical conservatives of a generation ago. This has happened frequently during the past hundred and fifty years, and though the present case seems more extreme, it need not in itself strike us unduly.

What is striking, however, is that very little music of importance written today adheres even approximately to traditional principles as they were still taught and accepted a generation ago. What we think of today as—let us use the word—"safe" music is relatively diatonic in conception; it is still based harmonically on the triad, very often with an added sixth or seventh or ninth; it sometimes is vaguely evocative of this or that style from the past; but its traditionalism seldom goes much farther than this. If a perfect cadence with a straightforward move from the dominant to the tonic occurs, it is not only the exception rather than the rule, but it has somewhat the effect of a stylization. The heavy texture of much late nineteenth and twentieth century music has most often given way to a linear counterpoint which may or may not rest on a strong harmonic foundation. If it does so, the harmonies which support the line are likely either to result, themselves, from essentially linear movement or to be simple and few, and often to be episodic rather than strongly constructive in effect.

I am talking technical jargon, of course, and my description is on the one hand incomplete, on the other general and composite. It refers to no single composer or even in a very precise sense to a single "style"; and I have no statistics, and know of none, by which my various statements could be checked. Who are the "conservative" composers, after all? What I have wanted to indicate, and this without going beyond what is already taken very much for granted, is the fact that in this period our musical ear is experiencing a fundamental change. By this I mean that not musicians only, but all those interested in music are feeling music differently and thinking in quite different terms from not only their predecessors of a generation back, but from the musicians and music lovers of many generations before the last one. New values are being created which embody these new modes of thought, and neither the modes of thought nor the values are any longer the exclusive possession of an "avant-garde." Another symptom of this change, possibly an even more convincing one, is to be seen in the status of musical theory and some aspects of musical education today. Clearly, questions of theory and education excite wide interest from all concerned with music. I spoke above of the number of books published with the listener's education in mind and ascribed that interest basically to the problems that have arisen through the fact that the listener is also the consumer. Yet that is not, I think, the entire reason. Another explanation, though not such an apparent one, for the number of popular books treating music analytically, lies, it seems to me, in the fact that, for two generations at least, traditional music theory has been under sharp scrutiny and not only by those identified with so-called "modern" music. This scrutiny has had two types of result: it has led to attempts either to formulate musical theory in entirely new terms, or to give traditional theory a new motivation and to lead it ahead to the point where a link with present-day practice becomes possible. It is furthermore striking, and most characteristic of our time, that composers have taken so large a part in this whole movement. For the first time in two hundred years, perhaps, many of the leading composers have become teachers, some of them outstanding ones. While this is undoubtedly partly the result of a change in the economic status of today's composers, it is partly also a result of the fact that in a transitional period like ours—that is, when traditional conceptions of musical theory are obviously no longer sufficient even as an approximate means of accounting for what the composer hears and writes—the composer is most likely to be the one to whom students of composition turn for guidance, and he is often impelled to formulate solutions of technical problems of which he has become aware in his own work. Actually, the roots of the technical crisis in music may be traced far back into the past. They may be traced, if one likes, at least to the time when Bach, following the implications of tonality to logical conclusions, advocated the general adoption of the tempered scale. This led, as we all know, to the exploitation of an ever wider circle of key relationships, and thus made possible the sonata form—what we call sometimes the "symphonic" technique of Beethoven. The essence of this technique is the possibility it yields of organizing the sharpest contrasts. It made possible not only, as I have pointed out previously, design of the largest possible span, by reason of the far-flung tonal relationships which it put at the composer's disposal, but it yielded also, quite inevitably, a far greater richness of detail on a smaller scale. For as bold juxtapositions of distantly related harmonies became familiar—as the ear became accustomed to them—it became inevitable that composers should use them with less and less constraint. We may regard the development of music in the nineteenth century as, from one point of view, the result of the fact that composers found such highly charged juxtapositions exciting and gained from them an apparently inexhaustible supply of new and even subtler nuances of expression. How many of Wagner's leitmotifs derive their expressive effect precisely from this (ex. 7).

But the examples I have given show only one aspect, and a relatively simple one, of this problem. For composers had learned also how to intensify harmonic effect through what is generally known as "alteration": the tension inherent in a given harmonic progression is heightened through the substitution of chromatic tones for diatonic ones. This method in some cases brings a tone closer to the one which follows it; in others it makes possible a contrast where originally a tone would have to be repeated. In many cases the

Die Walküre

Tristan

Götterdämmerung

Siegfried

(7)

tension is heightened through the fact that the altered tones produce dissonance.

Although the facts are familiar to all students of harmony, two very celebrated examples will help to make this clear:

(1) From Mozart's G minor Symphony:

which may be considered as, in a sense, derived from:

(2) From "Tristan":

which may be considered as, in the same sense, derived from:

I am not, of course, going to attempt to show you all the steps by which contemporary music, with all its problems, came into existence. I am actually speaking of only one aspect of the process, that of harmony, and even in harmony there were other factors besides those I have cited. My object here is simply to hint at the nature of the vast technical development by means of a few examples which have a certain consistency among themselves, even though they illus-trate only one phase of a much larger process. The point is that a mode of thought was developing which opened up constantly expanding possibilities and which was carried on through the force of its own logic and gathered momentum as the century progressed. This mode of musical thought—I trust that you re-member what I mean by that phrase—consists, as the above examples should make clear, in great concen-tration of tonal effect. Through the very logic of to-nality, as equal temperament allowed it to develop, it became possible to carry out in small detail processes similar to those discovered in the creation of larger design. It was this which seriously threatened the older bases of tonality. As of 1914—the year when the nine-teenth century began to collapse—the musical world (the creative musical world, that is) was dominated by Debussy and by Richard Strauss, whose music at that time seemed to carry the development of har-mony as far as it could be carried within the limits of the tonal system. Strauss had recently written his "Elek-tra," and it was not yet evident that in his later works he would turn his back decisively on the harmonic daring, and the expressive power, which that work em-bodies. As for Debussy, he at that time considered his work as in some sense an act of rebellion against the confining principles of tonality, widely regarded by the composers of that day as an encumbrance which had outlived its usefulness and of which composers had best rid themselves as quickly as possible.

The younger composers of that time—Schönberg, Bartok, and Stravinsky—were those who have given our period its character and have left music decisively changed from what it was before them. It is they who, in their several ways, have influenced the work of all later composers—even those who are opposed to them. It is not always thoroughly understood how the influence of a great artist takes effect. If the influence is at all profound it is by no means exerted only directly; it diffuses itself through the work of many lesser intermediaries and may be very noticeable even while the works of the master himself remain still unknown. It remains as a challenge to those who are repelled by it; and in the effort to meet the challenge they find themselves forced to come in some degree to terms with it. It is therefore above all these three composers (I know of no others of whom this can be said to be true in anything like the same degree) who have been the principal agents of the change; they have been the masculine forces, the fertilizing elements, that have brought it about. To say this is not, of course, to imply anything regarding the ultimate place which the history of music will assign to them. That we cannot know; it is not what concerns us, though it is true that it is precisely the composers who have molded their periods, who have left definitive and ineradicable imprints, who have been remembered afterwards.

It is, then, these composers above all who accomplished the revolution of which I spoke at the beginning of this chapter. I want to stress this fact because the next generation—my own—is not at all in the same sense a revolutionary one. It is rather one in which the materials yielded by the revolution must be assimilated anew and given new shapes; one in which the revolution must be appraised and consolidated, in which its various elements must be regrouped and its problems provided with fresh solutions. For the older generation was an extraordinary one; it not only posed the questions which contemporary music faces, it provided the first solutions of them.

The questions, of course, are those raised by revolution as such. Music had developed to a point where its formerly valid premises, of which tonality was only one, had collapsed; in a sense they had collapsed of their own weight. The nineteenth century had run its course, and composers were moved to discover new values to supersede it.

My subject here is music, not musicians, and I am not going to discuss the problems which this search for values implies in terms of the three composers mentioned. Their work is definitive, as are their answers to the problems; although two of them are still producing music which may well influence our final picture of them, their music is important in itself rather than as an embodiment of tendencies or points of view. The music is in all cases the embodiment of complex personalities, and it would be both primitive and misleading to regard it as primarily, or even to any important degree whatever, dogmatic in intent. One can never sufficiently stress the fact—vitally important but too often ignored in a period like our own—that it is the music itself, and not the type of music, which is important. Aesthetic points of view win their only valid victories through being embodied in great works of art; and the latter derive their greatness not from the aesthetic creeds embraced by those who created them, but by virtue of their own inherent qualities of imagination and of constructive order.

Let us then consider the problems of contemporary music not primarily from the critical nor yet from the historical point of view, but rather as a specific problem and in terms of varying reactions to that problem. These are perhaps the really fundamental questions; they are not primarily of a technical order at all, but rather questions of basic attitude, to which the technical problems are inevitably subordinate. A traditional order has to all intents and purposes lost its validity; it is still possible, but remains only one of many possibilities; it is no longer inevitable and in any case it is not capable of further development. Is music therefore essentially dead? And if not, what are the demands and the possibilities through which a new order, a new tradition, can be established? I trust I will be forgiven for not treating the first of these questions too seriously here. It is the kind of question which contains mortal dangers since its implications are far vaster than is visible at first sight. If we should allow ourselves to regard music as essentially dead— and we all know that there are those who choose to do so—we would be confessing not only our inability to cope with its demands, but our unwillingness to do so. We would be, as it were, denying our creative impulse or confessing ourselves devoid of it. As long as composers feel impelled to express themselves, music will be alive, and it is for us, with all the vitality at our disposal, to make it flourish.

But life implies development, and what has preoccupied composers is the means by which music can continue to develop. This has preoccupied them not in the abstract but in the concrete sense; they have been concerned, that is, with how to give to their own ideas the shape that the ideas demand. It was evident that the flood of new possibilities, or let us say new material, which music had acquired needed organization; that the nineteenth century development had led to a kind of anarchy for which the prevailing ideas of the time offered no principle of organization. The composers of the twenties felt very clearly that the freedom of resource they had acquired had been yielded ultimately by the classic tradition; that it had developed out of that tradition, which through its own inherent drive had led beyond itself. It was not a question of repudiating this tradition but of organizing the sequel to it.

In speaking of three general lines along which composers moved, I shall speak not so much of styles as of basic attitudes toward the problems in hand—of currents of thought which became ingredients of styles or personal "manners," and which have exerted their influence as such. They do, however, reflect differences in artistic philosophy which are not without significance; and possibly also they reflect basic human attitudes which run clearly parallel to some of those prevalent in our culture as a whole.

One such current of thought proposes, as it were, to consolidate a status quo on the basis of a modified and extended version of the older system. It has embodied itself in a searching critique of that system, from the point of view of contemporary practice, and has tried to formulate laws which will be as binding for the composers of today as the so-called rules of harmony and of strict counterpoint purported to be for the composers of the times in which they were written. It seems at times to go even farther than these, for whether the aforesaid rules were ever considered by those who formulated them to be so binding, they were actually never so in practice. But, simply because such a system essentially amounts to arresting a development in mid-course rather than, like the older systems, a compendium of data supplied by previous practice—for this very reason such a system is obliged to become rigid and, if I may be pardoned the term, authoritarian in conception. In effect it slams the door to certain developments, in the name of a necessarily vague conception of taste, a quality which is inherent and which cannot be inculcated by rule, any more, in fact, than genius can be. And while at best such a conception may possess real validity for one composer, or a single group of composers who are his followers, it is bound almost inexorably to seem arbitrary and restrictive to others. In attempting to arrest movement it inevitably turns out to be reactionary; and in fact it may well be in some of its aspects the essentially reactionary tendency of today.

The second current is subtler. It seeks outspoken contacts with the past as a point of departure for a new and severe logic of a radically diatonic type. It does not so much close the door on the developments I have spoken of as by-pass them; it even utilizes them on occasion for its own rigorous ends and at its best has achieved rather remarkable feats of synthesis and of style. It is less essentially reactionary than the first tendency in that it leaves the way open, by implication at least, for further development and synthesis even while implicitly opposing other solutions. I find it, however, extremely problematical in two respects. First of all, it is artificial in that its points of departure are arbitrary even if its restrictions are not. There is nothing in diatonicism that is inherently sacrosanct. It is one of the forms which musical thought has taken but which has been extended and enriched in its implications by chromatic elaborations, ever since the beginnings of tonality. And in by-passing, as I have said, chromatic implications of a radical sort, it by-passes also the principles on which classic tonality was based. It is for this reason that such music seems often static and inflexible, for it is based on a diatonicism which is actually far more radical, because it is self-conscious, than the diatonicism of, say, Mozart or Bach.

The second objection has to do with the fact that in turning for contacts to the past, one is forced to distort that past. The past is never, as our jargon implies, a fixed quantity; it is, as I pointed out earlier, in movement. If we regard it clearly, we see it moving toward us, and if we set out to meet it, we find that it sees itself quite differently from the way we see it. Mozart for his contemporaries was not the serene classic, the apostle of measure and perfection, that so many of his admirers of the nineteenth century, and even some of those of today, have liked to conjure up. On the contrary, he was for them a painter of intense and even somber canvases, of large scope and vast design, whom Lorenzo da Ponte is said on one occasion to have coupled in comparison with Dante of the *Inferno*.

There is of course another current—the most dangerous and the most difficult, but perhaps the most fruitful, since its essential element is that it accepts all of the implications of what we may call the tonal revolution and seeks to organize them on a basis that is really inherent in their nature, and in a way that involves no contradiction or distortion of the past. To fully understand it, full conversance with tradition is indispensable, since one cannot fully grasp the nature of the tonal revolution unless one is aware, at least in one's ear, of what has led to it. Once more I am not speaking of a specific technique—this is a matter for the composer—but of an attitude. I find, too, that only obstacles have been created by the general traffic in such a term as "atonality," which is obviously associated primarily with the current I am speaking of but which actually means nothing, even though certain composers have adopted it as a kind of definitive slogan. "Atonality" implies the denial of tonality; but the facts, as I have tried to show, represent a tonal supersaturation. One could rather speak, then, of supersaturated tonality, and possibly speak of "post-tonal" rather than "a-tonal" music. Its technical principles, as a matter of fact, have not yet been definitely formulated. The much misunderstood twelve-tone technique, or twelve-tone system, represents one answer to certain of the problems it raises and has, as is well known, provided a whole group of composers (including not only Schönberg but some of the most gifted among later ones) with a point of departure for some of the finest of contemporary works. I shall not try to describe or to discuss the system here. I have not in fact ever adopted it myself in any thorough-going manner, though I shall do so without hesitation if I ever feel that it provides the answer to my particular problems. But I feel most strongly that the music is most readily understood if the technique is forgotten; one must always listen, as to all music, with open ears, and try to hear its sounds and absorb them as such, with no conscious effort whatever.

This brings us once again to the problem of artist and public, and also to the problem, already referred to, of the artist's autonomy. As I have said, these changes have been brought about by the artist. They are the very life of music; they go to the very roots of our culture since they are only the musical equivalents —self-sufficient but deeply and, if you wish, mysteriously connected with the rest of life—of the changes that have taken place in the world as a whole. Need I insist on this point? Music changes as the whole of culture changes, because we are still in the midst of the technological revolution and the inner and outer adjustments which the technological revolution demands of us. Thus, while we find music in the midst of a technical crisis in which composers are preoccupied with new sound-relationships, and very much aware of the problems which these new sound-relationships raise for them, we find also that the world in general is simultaneously in the midst of a semantic crisis; words have radically acquired new meanings and new associations, and we are thus acutely conscious of the details of our very language.

But just as it is musicians who have brought about these changes, we must insist, above all, on the autonomy of the artist, and resist with the greatest energy all those who, whether incited by totalitarian movements or by the pressures of large-scale economy, would press for limitations of that autonomy. Without this complete freedom for the artist to create according to his impulses, there can be no development. Music, or any art, can in such a case only follow the law of the lowest common denominator; in providing the public with "what it wants" it will inexorably tend to provide it with what is understood with least effort. Under such conditions, music ceases to be vital experience and becomes a mere amusement or, as totalitarian governments seem to wish, a drug.

This is not intended as a plea for what is generally called "l'art pour l'art"—certainly not as a slogan. Artistic values remain, and remain in the last analysis, identical with human ones. We must ask of the artist what we ask of human beings in general, and assign to him values that are of general relevance. If we call him great it will be because he concerns himself with real issues, not with false ones; and when art is trivial, the result of mere exhibitionism, of mere navel-gazing, we will label it as such. But the cause of art is furthered sometimes by unexpected means, and we will beware of shallow judgments.

Finally, what of our American situation? I said before that the rather gloomy picture I painted of the effect of large-scale economy was not the whole story. If it were, the outlook would be quite hopeless. The nature of the whole set of facts I have been describing would give us additional and final reason for gloom. For how is our musical public ever to make a real contact with the music of our time when everything in our public musical life tends, since it is based so largely on such premises as are obtained from sales charts and opinion polls, to make the music even more inacessible? The answer to this question is, I think, to be found in the ever-increasing awareness of music apparent everywhere. It is in our schools, our universities, our choral societies, in the numerous local activities of individuals and sometimes small and even unpretentious groups of individuals, all over the country, who demand musical experience that is vital and who exert themselves to offer and to demand it. They are, in effect, by-passing the large scale business enterprise of music, and will no doubt more and more learn to make real demands on it, productive of real changes. It is these that we must, above all, support, and on them we must pin our hopes.

Roger Sessions

ROGER H. SESSIONS, composer and Conant Professor of
Music at Princeton University, was born at Brooklyn
in 1896. Educated at Harvard and Yale, he has taught
music in a number of institutions but principally at
Princeton and the University of California. His compositions, many of them commissioned, include four
symphonies, three string quartets, an opera (*The Trial
of Lucullus*), concertos for violin and for piano and
orchestra, chorales for organ, sonatas, choral works.
They have received numerous awards, among them
prizes of the Naumberg Foundation, the Critics Circle,
Brandeis University, and the Gold Medal of the
National Institute of Arts and Letters.